Daily Prayers

FOR

Church of England People

THE DEFINITIVE EDITION

Compiled by

HARRY OGDEN

Foreword by
BISHOP JACK NICHOLLS
former Bishop of Sheffield

This edition published in Great Britain in 2010

Society for Promoting Christian Knowledge
36 Causton Street
London SW1P 4ST

British Library Cataloguing-in-Publication Data
A catalogue record for this book is available from the British Library

ISBN 978–0–281–06200–3

1 3 5 7 9 10 8 6 4 2

Designed and typeset by Kenneth Burnley, Wirral, Cheshire
Printed in Great Britain by Ashford Colour Press

Produced on paper from sustainable forests

Contents

Foreword

Harry Ogden is one of the unsung heroes of the Church of England. I first met him almost forty years ago when he was a parish priest in one of the poorest areas of Manchester. He began his ministry in such a parish and served for the whole of his working life in such areas, where he devoted himself to the worship of GOD and the care of GOD 's people. To offer the best to GOD has always been his life's work. The buildings in which he offered the Liturgy were made beautiful so as to lift the heart to GOD. He knows in his bones that worship, both public and private, is the heartbeat of the Church. It overflows into the service of all people, especially the poor. The pages which follow are the result of that life and vision. There is nothing better to put into the hands of the newly confirmed or of anyone who would have something simple, practical and yet profound to help them in their journey into GOD.

The Rt Revd Jack Nicholls
Former Bishop of Sheffield

In loving memory of my parents,

Harry and Mary Ogden,

my paternal great-grandmother,

Sarah Ellen Jones,

in whose house I was born,
my maternal grandmother,

Mary Anne Halls,

my uncles,

Frank and Walter Halls

The LORD gave: the LORD has taken away:
Blessed be the name of the LORD

See Job 1.21

May they rest in the peace of CHRIST
As they await His joyful resurrection

About this book

Some Daily Prayers for Church of England People is a book of *personal* prayers for private use, which can be read or memorized to focus our hearts and minds on the ONE and only GOD – FATHER, SON and HOLY SPIRIT. They are old and new – some from the Holy Bible, the official daily public worship of the Church of England and other Churches, or those of fellow Christians from different times and places. In this way our personal daily prayer is 'tuned in' to the worship offered to GOD THE SACRED TRINITY by the whole Catholic Church all over the world and in heaven, at all times without ceasing.

The book is in five parts:

1 'Daily prayers', which take about three minutes or so each day.

2 'Various things to pray and ponder' provides for various moods and needs. You can use these Godly reminders at Morning or Night Prayers or at other times to suit yourself.

3 'God's forgiveness' provides the way to be honest with GOD about yourself and seek His forgiveness. You will never get very far in following JESUS unless you are prepared to be completely honest with Him, and let Him serve you by washing away all your sins.

4 'At the Eucharist' provides personal prayers for use before the service begins, before and after going to the altar to meet and receive OUR LORD JESUS CHRIST in Holy Communion, and at the end of the service before you go out with Him to serve Him in your everyday life.

5 'The Christian hope': The Coming of Christ, Last Judgement and Resurrection to Life Everlasting.

By praying briefly and systematically each day you will not catch religious mania – but you will keep close to GOD IN CHRIST, which is what Christianity is about.

LORD GOD, You have made us for Yourself,
and our hearts are restless,
until they find their rest in You.   St Augustine of Hippo (d. 430)

I came that they may have life,
life in all its fullness.   See John 10.10

Explanation, instruction and comment about prayer and praying are shown in italic text.

Abbreviations and glossary

Anglican	To do with the Church of England and its sister Churches throughout the world
ASB	*The Alternative Service Book 1980*
AV	Authorized (King James) Version of the Bible
BCP	The Book of Common Prayer
CHN	The Community of the Holy Name, Derby, an Anglican religious community for women in England and southern Africa
CR	Community of the Resurrection, Mirfield, an Anglican religious community for men in England and formerly also in southern Africa and the West Indies
CW	*Common Worship*
CW^1	*Services and Prayers for the Church of England*
CW^2	*Daily Prayer*
CW^3	*Times and Seasons*
CW^4	*Pastoral Services*
CW^5	*Christian Initiation*
GNB	Good News Bible
HO	Harry Ogden, the compiler/author of this book
Incarnation	Christ who has always been God also became one of us when He was born by the Holy Spirit of the Virgin Mary, so that He is God and humanity united
NIV	New International Version of the Bible
NRSV	New Revised Standard Version of the Bible
RSV	Revised Standard Version of the Bible
SSC	The Society of the Sacred Cross, Tymawr Convent, Gwent, an Anglican religious community for women

Christian duties

Being a Christian means accepting JESUS CHRIST as Lord and Saviour. This necessarily involves being a living part or member of His Body the CHURCH – the Body He uses now to continue His work of glorifying GOD our Father; spreading the Good News of His gospel throughout the world, and saving all humankind. Nobody can be a Christian on their own, isolated from JESUS in His Body the Church.

A Christian has certain obligations to Him in His Church. These are some of them:

1 Worship GOD at the Eucharist wherever you are on all *Sundays* and other main *Holy Days* (page 84).

2 Receive Holy Communion always at *Easter, Whitsunday and Christmas*, and regularly at other times – after careful preparation (page 85).

3 Pray wherever you are every day (pages 1–24).

4 Be honest with GOD about yourself and your sins and seek His forgiveness, when necessary by going to confession (pages 73–82).

5 Fast on *Ash Wednesday* and *Good Friday* (page 26).

6 Read the good news in the Bible, particularly the New Testament, at least once a week, if not more often.

7 Give money, as much as you can afford, to pay your fair share of providing for GOD's work through His Church and clergy, and for charitable work.

The earliest Christians continued steadfast:

• in the *apostles' teaching* and *fellowship*;

• in the *Breaking of Bread* (the Eucharist);

• and *the prayers*.

See Acts 2.42.

An invitation

Come now,
put aside your busy-ness for a while,
take refuge for a time
from your troublesome thoughts:
throw away your cares,
and let your burdensome worries wait.

Take some time off for GOD:
rest for a while in Him.

Enter the secret room of your mind,
put out everything except GOD,
and whatever helps you to find Him.
Close the door of your mind,
and seek GOD.

Say *now* to GOD
with all your heart,
'I seek Your face, LORD:
Your face I seek.'   St Anselm (d. 1109), 36th Archbishop of Canterbury (adapted)

Retire my Friend, and meditate, and see
how gracious GOD hath been to thee and me.
Tho' People did Both thee and me deride,
yet Trust thy GOD, and He'll for thee provide.

From the tombstone of John Ashworth (d. 1793),
in the churchyard of Saint Nicholas, Newchurch in Rossendale

GOD is first and foremost that depth around all things and beyond all things into which, when I pray, I try to sink. But GOD is also the activity that comes to me out of that depth, tells me I'm loved, that opens up a future for me, that offers transformations I can't imagine. Very much a mystery but also very much a presence. Very much a person.

Rowan Williams, 104th Archbishop of Canterbury

About prayer

JESUS said:

Keep watch, and *pray* . . . The spirit is willing, but the flesh is weak.

Mark 14.38, GNB

'Secret' is a good word to describe that prayer which rises from the heart to GOD when we are alone by ourselves . . . '*Pray to your Father* who is in the secret place, and He will reward you' . . . GOD is not an abstract principle or an impersonal absolute, but One whose intense personal love cares for every individual person. He is present in this secret place. However sad, forlorn, self-despising a man may feel himself to be when he thinks only of himself and looks inwardly upon himself, GOD is present in the fullness of intimate love to comfort loneliness and redeem solitude . . . [Prayer] is not a dialogue between a madman and his shadow, but heart-to-heart communion between *the child of GOD* . . . and *the Father, the Holy Being*, who watches over them, and hears and answers them when they pray.

Hedley Hodkin (d. 1995), Canon of Manchester

If the Christian ceases to pray, to long for GOD, to know the presence of CHRIST, then he becomes like salt that has lost its taste. Religion then degenerates into convention and respectability, behind which timid souls seek to escape life.

Anon.

Prayer is not simply about seeking divine help and intervention. It has more to do with being in tune with GOD's will, by offering Him adoration, confession and thanksgiving. On this basis, supplication is possible: not for personal gain, or to make GOD change His mind, but to provide a channel through which His loving purpose for creation may become reality.

Stephen Smalley, Dean of Chester, 2001

Love to pray – feel often during the day the need for prayer, and take trouble to pray. Prayer enlarges the heart until it is capable of containing GOD's gift of himself. Ask and seek, and your heart will grow big enough to receive him . . .
Mother Teresa of Calcutta (d. 1997)

I offer praise and thanks to GOD
not for anything I may gain by it
but because He is good beyond all telling,
and He is mine and I am His.
Jack Winslow (d. 1974), Anglican priest and spiritual guide

On the helpfulness of ikons

From early times it came to be believed that our faith could be expressed in pictures as well as in words. The Ten Commandments had forbidden any attempt to depict GOD, and truly the mystery of GOD is beyond both words and pictures. But since GOD was and is revealed in JESUS CHRIST, one can depict His humanity, His life and His friends.

Such pictures ('ikon' is simply the Greek word for 'image' or 'likeness') are not only reminders of GOD and the gospel, but also vehicles through which we turn our attention to GOD and are drawn to prayer, and through which GOD touches us and blesses us with Divine love and attention.

Theresa Margaret CHN

DAILY PRAYERS

Short morning prayers

✠ In the name of the FATHER, and of the SON,
And of the HOLY SPIRIT. Amen.

The Gathering, Holy Communion, Order One, CW [1]

GOD, you are my GOD, early I will seek You,
My soul thirsts for You, my flesh longs for You,
in a barren and dry land where no water is.

See Psalm 63

Holy GOD,
holy and strong,   (three times)
holy and immortal,
have mercy upon us.

Confessions, CW [1]

Our FATHER, who art in heaven, hallowed be Thy name:
Thy kingdom come, Thy will be done,
on earth as it is in heaven.
Give us this day our daily bread.
And forgive us our trespasses,
as we forgive those who trespass against us.
And lead us not into temptation,
but deliver us from evil.
For Thine is the kingdom, the power and the glory
for ever and ever. Amen.

Holy Communion, Order One (traditional version), CW [1]

Glory to the FATHER and to the SON, and to the HOLY SPIRIT:
as it was in the beginning, is now, and shall be for ever. Amen.

An Order for Night Prayer (Compline), CW [1]

FATHER, thank You for keeping me safe last night:
and for giving me this new day.
May I glorify You by showing Your love to all I meet,
and serving You to the best of my ability,
at home, at work, at pleasure, and at prayer,
in the power of the SPIRIT,
and in union with CHRIST. Amen.   HO

Bless all whom I love, the living and the departed . . .
all I shall meet today; and keep us safe.
May Blessed Mary and all the Saints surround us
with their strong and loving prayers. Amen.   HO

The ✠ grace of our LORD JESUS CHRIST, the love of GOD,
and the fellowship of the HOLY SPIRIT, be with us all evermore. Amen.

Endings and Blessings, *CW* [1]

Short night prayers

✠ In the name of the FATHER, and of the SON,
And of the HOLY SPIRIT. Amen.

The Gathering, Holy Communion, Order One, *CW* [1]

O LORD, let my prayer be in Your sight as the incense:
the lifting up of my hands as the evening sacrifice.   See Psalm 141

LORD, have mercy: CHRIST, have mercy: LORD, have mercy.

Our FATHER, who art in heaven, hallowed be Thy name:
Thy kingdom come, Thy will be done,
on earth as it is in heaven.
Give us this day our daily bread.
And forgive us our trespasses,
as we forgive those who trespass against us.
And lead us not into temptation,
but deliver us from evil.
For Thine is the kingdom, the power and the glory
for ever and ever. Amen.

Holy Communion, Order One (traditional version), *CW* [1]

Glory to the FATHER and to the SON, and to the HOLY SPIRIT:
as it was in the beginning, is now, and shall be for ever. Amen.

An Order for Night Prayer (Compline), *CW* [1]

FATHER,
Thank You for all Your blessings today . . .
Forgive all my sins . . . I am truly sorry;
Bless my family and friends wherever they are,
living and departed . . .
Bless all in any need or trouble . . .
Bless all I have wronged . . . , all who have wronged me . . . ,
and give us a forgiving spirit:
Bless me, Your unworthy servant:
I leave You with my hopes . . . , and fears . . . ,
for You know what is best for me:
All these things I ask in the power of the SPIRIT,
and in union with CHRIST. Amen.   HO

May Blessed Mary, (St . . .) and all Your saints
surround us with their strong and loving prayers. Amen.

May GOD THE SACRED TRINITY
✠ FATHER, SON and HOLY SPIRIT,
bless and protect us this night
and keep us all in life eternal. Amen.

The Lord's Prayer

JESUS said:

When you pray, say 'Our FATHER . . .'

Not a day has passed in nearly two thousand years when this prayer has not been said, and said in every conceivable situation, by people of all ages and in every nation and in every kind of mood: thankfully, resignedly, thoughtlessly, anxiously, dutifully out of habit, trustingly in pain and in sickness, and at the point of death. 'LORD, teach us to pray', His friends had said to JESUS. And what He does is not simply to tell them how to pray but to give them a prayer which will form a bond of unity between them and among all Christians ever after: a kind of signature tune, if you like: all we will ever need to express our trusting relationship with GOD and our dependence on Him.

Michael Mayne (d. 2006), Dean of Westminster, 1986–1996

If you fail to say the Morning and Night Prayers, then at least say the LORD'S PRAYER as JESUS told us to do.

The Jesus Prayer

LORD JESUS CHRIST, SON OF GOD:
have mercy on me a sinner.

The JESUS PRAYER is basically an adaptation of the prayer of the blind man at Jericho (Luke 18.38) and the prayer of the publican (Luke 18.13). Eastern Christians repeat it frequently and silently each day as a means of maintaining a continual awareness of GOD. A prayer using words, it is a means of focusing on GOD in silent adoration.

It is a short, direct, simple prayer which is easy to remember and use – even in difficult circumstances, when other forms of prayer become difficult. It needs to be repeated frequently over and over again – and can be used as a means of intercession, 'Have mercy on (him, her, them, us)', as well as for oneself.

It can be said in tune with breathing – breathe in during the first part addressed to JESUS, and breathe out during the second part. HO

Those who live very near to JESUS grow like Him . . . The secret of the saints is 'keeping our eyes fixed on JESUS'.

Brother Edward (d. 1953), Anglican priest and spiritual guide

More morning prayers

✠ In the power of the SPIRIT, and in union with CHRIST,
I pray to the FATHER.

Forms of Intercession, Holy Communion (adapted), *CW* [1]

I will exalt You, O GOD, my King
And I will praise Your name for ever and ever.
Every day will I give thanks unto You,
And praise Your name for ever and ever.

See Psalm 145

LORD, have mercy: CHRIST, have mercy: LORD, have mercy.

Our FATHER, who art in heaven, hallowed be Thy name:
Thy kingdom come, Thy will be done,
on earth as it is in heaven.
Give us this day our daily bread.
And forgive us our trespasses,
as we forgive those who trespass against us.
And lead us not into temptation,
but deliver us from evil.
For Thine is the kingdom, the power and the glory
for ever and ever. Amen.

Holy Communion, Order One (traditional version), *CW* [1]

Glory to the FATHER, through the SON, in the HOLY SPIRIT:
Three persons equal in majesty, undivided in splendour,
yet ONE GOD, ever to be worshipped and adored
by all the hosts of heaven, by all mankind,
by all living creatures, and by the whole creation.
Blessing and honour and glory and power
be Yours for ever and ever. Amen.   HO and various

My GOD, I am not my own but Yours.
I give myself to You,
     in joy and in sorrow,
     in sickness and in health,
     in success and in failure,
     in life and in death,
     in time and for eternity.

Almighty and everlasting FATHER
we thank You that You have brought us safely
     to the beginning of this day.
Keep us from falling into sin
     or running into danger:
order us in all our doings
and guide us to do always what is right in Your eyes:
through JESUS CHRIST OUR LORD. Amen.

Collect for Morning Prayer on Wednesdays, *CW* [2]

Bless all whom I love, the living and the departed . . .
all I shall meet today; and keep us safe.
May Blessed Mary and all the Saints surround us
with their strong and loving prayers. Amen.   HO

Hail Mary (see opposite).

The ✠ grace of our LORD JESUS CHRIST, the love of GOD,
and the fellowship of the HOLY SPIRIT, be with us all evermore. Amen.

Endings and Blessings, *CW* [1]

The Hail Mary

(Luke 1.28, 42)

Hail Mary, full of grace, the LORD is with you.
Blessed are you among women,
and blessed is the fruit of your womb, JESUS.
Holy Mary, Mother of GOD, pray for us sinners
now and at the hour of our death.

The first part of the Hail Mary is adapted from Saint Luke's Gospel. It is a joyful reminder that the Incarnation (Jesus who had always been GOD, also becoming one of us) is the most wonderful event in history: and that GOD used one of us, the Virgin Mary, as His means of doing this.

The second part is a reminder that CHRIST has abolished our loneliness, that we pray (even if alone at home or in an empty church) within the fabulous community of CHRIST'S family the Church, that we live in this Family, and owe more to it than we realize – and that we particularly rely on the prayers of other members of His Family, especially His Saints in heaven, of whom the blessed Virgin Mary, His Mother, is the representative figure.

Adapted from Five for Sorrow, Ten for Joy
by the Revd Neville Ward, a Methodist minister

Virgin Mary, full of grace,
who gave birth
    to our LORD and SAVIOUR JESUS CHRIST
with all generations we call you blessed
and with you the whole Church in earth and heaven
we praise and magnify His holy Name.
Pray for us, Bearer of the eternal WORD,
    with all the Saints and faithful departed,
        now and always.   HO

Also the Angelus, pages 23–4.

More night prayers

☧ In the power of the SPIRIT, and in union with CHRIST,
I pray to the FATHER.

Forms of Intercession, Holy Communion (adapted), *CW* [1]

Most Holy and Glorious TRINITY,
FATHER, SON and HOLY SPIRIT,
Three Persons in ONE GOD.
I believe that You are present here,
and with all my heart and soul I worship and adore You. Amen.   Anon.

LORD, have mercy: CHRIST, have mercy: LORD, have mercy.

Our FATHER, who art in heaven, hallowed be Thy name:
Thy kingdom come, Thy will be done,
on earth as it is in heaven.
Give us this day our daily bread.
And forgive us our trespasses,
as we forgive those who trespass against us.
And lead us not into temptation,
but deliver us from evil.
For Thine is the kingdom, the power and the glory
for ever and ever. Amen.

Holy Communion, Order One (traditional version), *CW* [1]

Look back –

> *Who have I wronged or hurt in any way?*
> *What have I thought wrong?*
> *What have I said wrong?*
> *What have I done wrong?*
> *What have I failed to do?*

Have mercy on me, O GOD, after Your great goodness;
for I acknowledge my faults, and my sin is ever before me.
Turn Your face from all my sins, make me a clean heart, O GOD,
and renew a right spirit within me.
See Psalm 51

May CHRIST bring me wholeness of body, mind and spirit.
Deliver ✠ me from all my sins and from every evil,
and give me His peace. Amen.
Thanksgiving for the Healing Ministry of the Church (adapted), *CW* [1]

Lighten our darkness, LORD we pray;
and in Your mercy defend us
from all perils and dangers of this night;
for the love of Your only SON,
our Saviour JESUS CHRIST. Amen.
Collect for Evening Prayer on Sunday, *CW* [2]

Use one or more of the following as needed:

FATHER, I thank You
for my creation, preservation
and all the blessings of this life (especially . . .),
for the redemption of the world by Our LORD JESUS CHRIST;
and for the means of grace and hope of Glory
given to us in His Body the Church.
    And give me such a sense of all Your mercies
that my heart may be truly thankful,
and that I show forth Your praise,
not only with my lips but in my life,
by giving up myself to Your service,
and by walking before You
in holiness and righteousness all my days,
through JESUS CHRIST our LORD, Amen.
General Thanksgiving (adapted), BCP

LORD, bless my family and friends, living and departed . . .
all who are sick or in any need or trouble . . .
all involved in disaster, war or persecution . . .
all I have wronged . . . or who have wronged me . . .
LORD, have mercy.

GOD grant to the living grace, to the departed rest,
to the Church, the Queen, the Commonwealth and all people
  unity, peace and concord,
and to me and all His servants life everlasting,
through CHRIST our Saviour. Amen.

An Order of Service for Remembrance Sunday, CW [3]

Personal Prayers (page 27).

Petitions (page 32).

Hail Mary (page 9).

The LORD almighty grant us a quiet night and a perfect end.

An Order for Night Prayer (Compline), CW [1]

Save us, O LORD, while waking,
and guard us while sleeping,
that awake we may watch with CHRIST
and asleep we may rest in peace.

Antiphon to Nunc Dimittis, Compline, CW [1]

May the infinite and glorious TRINITY,
the ✠ FATHER, the SON, and the HOLY SPIRIT,
direct my life in good works,
and after my journey through this world,
grant me eternal rest with the saints, and all whom I love. Amen.

Blessings and other Endings, Funerals (adapted), CW [4]

Prayers during the day

A weekly cycle of Daily Worship expressing the faith of the Church

And the Catholick faith is this, that we **worship** *ONE GOD IN TRINITY and TRINITY IN UNITY.*   Creed of St Athanasius, BCP

The weekly cycle of worship provides a short 'daily office' for each working day. It begins each day with a psalm or canticle or hymn, a short Bible reading, and a suitable prayer that relates to a basic Christian belief.

No more than three minutes or so are needed each day to say these appointed prayers – but this can be expanded by a longer period of silent concentration on GOD.

You can say these Worship Prayers each day at any time to suit your circumstances. This could be early morning before work, on a bus, after the children have gone to school, in a church, during the mid-day meal break, after work, during a rest break on a car journey, and so on.

Now turn to the appropriate day of the week.

The Faith of the Church

I believe in GOD, THE FATHER ALMIGHTY,
creator of heaven and earth.

I believe in JESUS CHRIST, HIS ONLY SON, OUR LORD.
He was conceived by the power of the HOLY SPIRIT
and born of the Virgin Mary.
He suffered under Pontius Pilate,
was crucified, died, and was buried.
He descended to the dead.
On the third day He rose again.
He ascended into heaven,
and is seated at the right hand of the FATHER.
He will come again to judge the living and the dead.

I believe in the HOLY SPIRIT,
the holy catholic Church,
the communion of saints,
the forgiveness of sins,
the resurrection of the body,
and the life everlasting. Amen.   The Apostles' Creed, *ASB*

We have no doctrine of our own – we only possess the Catholic doctrine of the Catholic Church enshrined in the Catholic Creeds, and those Creeds we hold without addition or diminution . . .

The Church of England was in existence long before the Reformation, and while it was deeply affected by the travails of the Reformation, it emerged from them in all essential respects the same Church as before within the One Catholic and Apostolic Church.

Geoffrey Fisher (d. 1972), 99th Archbishop of Canterbury, 1945–1961

We hold the Catholic Faith in its entirety: that is to say, the truth of CHRIST, contained in Holy Scripture: stated in the . . . Creeds: expressed in the Sacraments . . . : safeguarded by the historical three-fold Order of Ministry.

Our Bishops at the 1930 Lambeth Conference

Sundays

Wherever you are:
Worship GOD at the EUCHARIST, also called
HOLY COMMUNION, MASS or LORD'S SUPPER.

A hundred welcomes to You,
O KING of the Blessed Sunday
who comes with help to us after the week.
Stir up my feet to Holy Eucharist.
Stir up my lips to blessed speech.
Stir up my heart and banish spite from it.
I look up to the Son of Mary,
to her only Son of Mercy,
for He has so wonderfully redeemed us
and alive or dead we belong to Him.   Irish Gaelic prayer (adapted)

The Lord's Own Service
for the Lord's Own People
every Lord's Day

The shortage of priests in some areas does not always allow for the Eucharist to
be celebrated every Sunday in every local church. Where this is so, we should be
ready to travel, if at all possible, to the nearest church where the Eucharist is to
be celebrated. Although in a different place, it will be the same Eucharist and
the same SAVIOUR who is present, who invites us, and who is expecting us. He
said 'Do this'.

Also page 83.

Mondays

God the Sacred Trinity

This is the faith of the Church. This is my faith.
We believe and trust in ONE GOD,
FATHER, SON and HOLY SPIRIT.

Authorized Affirmation of Faith (adapted), *CW* [1]

A Song of the Church

We praise You, O GOD:
we acclaim You as the LORD;
all creation worships You:
the FATHER everlasting.
To You all angels, all the powers of heaven,
the cherubim and seraphim, sing in endless praise:
Holy, holy, holy LORD, GOD of power and might,
heaven and earth are full of Your glory.
The glorious company of the apostles praise You.
The noble fellowship of prophets praise You.
The white-robed army of martyrs praise You.
Throughout the world, the holy Church proclaims You:
FATHER, of majesty unbounded:
Your true and only SON, worthy of all praise,
The HOLY SPIRIT, advocate and guide.

Te Deum: Part 1, Other Canticles, CW [1]

Reading:

I bow my knees before the FATHER . . . I pray that, according to the
riches of His glory, He may grant that you may be strengthened in
your inner being with power through His SPIRIT and that CHRIST
may dwell in your hearts through faith, as you are being rooted and
grounded in love.   Ephesians 3.14, 16, 17, NRSV

Glory to the FATHER, through the SON, in the HOLY SPIRIT:
Three persons equal in majesty, undivided in splendour,
    yet ONE GOD, ever to be worshipped and adored
by all the hosts of heaven, by all mankind,
by all living creatures, and by the whole creation.
Blessing and honour and glory and power
be Yours for ever and ever. Amen.   HO and various

LORD GOD, You have made us for Yourself,
and our hearts are restless,
until they find their rest in You.   St Augustine of Hippo (d. 430)

Also pages 54–5.

Tuesdays

God, the Father Almighty,
creator of heaven and earth

Venite:

O come let us sing unto the LORD:
   let us heartily rejoice in the strength of our salvation.
Let us come before His presence with thanksgiving:
   and show ourselves glad in Him with psalms.
For the LORD is a great GOD:
   and a great King above all gods:
In His hand are all the corners of the earth:
   and the strength of the hills is His also.
The sea is His and He made it:
   and His hands prepared the dry land.
O come, let us worship and bow down:
   and kneel before the LORD OUR MAKER.
For He is the LORD OUR GOD:
   and we are the people of His pasture, and the sheep of His hand.
Today, if ye will hear His voice, harden not your hearts.

Psalm 95, BCP

Glory to the FATHER and to the SON, and to the HOLY SPIRIT:
As it was in the beginning, is now, and shall be for ever. Amen.

An Order for Night Prayer (Compline), CW [1]

Reading:

In the beginning, LORD, You created the earth, and the heavens are
the work of Your hands: they will perish but You remain: they will all
grow old like a garment. Like a cloak You will roll them up and they
will be changed. But You are the same, and Your years will never end.

See Hebrews 1.10–12

Most high and HOLY ONE,
Maker of all that is,
on earth and on the myriads of stars and planets and galaxies
   far beyond in outer space:
may we be filled with awe and wonder

at the endless splendour and the majesty of Your whole creation;
and find fulfilment in You, with all You have made:
our Maker, our Saviour and our Enabler,
FATHER, SON and HOLY SPIRIT. Amen.   HO

You are worthy, our LORD and GOD,
to receive glory and honour and power;
for You created all things
and by Your will they were created and have their being.

Revelation 4.11, NIV

Also pages 41–2.

Wednesdays

God the Holy Spirit

Veni Creator Spiritus:

Come, HOLY GHOST, our souls inspire,
And lighten with celestial fire:
Thou the anointing SPIRIT art,
Who dost thy sevenfold gifts impart.

Thy blessed unction from above
Is comfort, life, and fire of love;
Enable with perpetual light
The dullness of our blinded sight.

Anoint and cheer our soiled face
With the abundance of Thy grace:
Keep far our foes, give peace at home;
Where Thou art guide no ill can come.

Teach us to know the FATHER, SON,
And THEE, of Both, to be but ONE;
That through the ages all along
This may be our endless song,
    'Praise to Thy eternal merit,
    FATHER, SON and HOLY SPIRIT.'

Veni Creator Spiritus, A Form of Preparation for Holy Communion, *CW* [1]

Reading:

The fruit of the SPIRIT is *love, joy, peace, long-suffering, kindness, goodness, faithfulness, meekness, self-control* . . . They that are of CHRIST JESUS have crucified the flesh with its passions and lusts.

See Galatians 5.22, 24

HOLY SPIRIT, re-make me in all my ways,
   outwardly and inwardly,
     like CHRIST.
May His likeness be in my face
   – not for my own pride, glory or vanity
   – but so that others can see
what the loving presence of CHRIST can do
when He is received into the heart of a sinner
     like me.
May CHRIST be real to others, through me. Amen.   HO

Come, HOLY SPIRIT, fill the hearts of Your faithful people,
and kindle in us the fire of Your love.

Responsory from Morning Prayer: Ascension until Pentecost, *CW*[2]

Also pages 52–3.

Thursdays

Jesus Christ our Saviour – God and Man

The Song of Christ's Glory

CHRIST JESUS was in the form of GOD
   but He did not cling to equality with GOD.
He emptied Himself, taking the form of a servant,
   and was born in our human likeness.
Being found in human form He humbled Himself,
   and became obedient unto death, even death on a cross;
Therefore, GOD has highly exalted Him,
   and bestowed on Him the Name above every name,

That at the NAME OF JESUS every knee shall bow,
in heaven and on earth and under the earth.
And every tongue confess that JESUS CHRIST IS LORD,
to the glory of GOD THE FATHER.   Philippians 2.5–11

Glory to the FATHER and to the SON, and to the HOLY SPIRIT:
As it was in the beginning, is now, and shall be for ever. Amen.
                    The Song of Christ's Glory, Canticles, *CW* [1]

Reading:

GOD so loved the world that He gave His only SON, so that whoever
believes in Him shall not perish but have everlasting life. Indeed, GOD
did not send His SON into the world to condemn the world, but in
order that the world might be saved through Him.

                                        See John 3.16–17

Blessed be GOD.
Blessed be His holy Name.
Blessed be JESUS CHRIST, true GOD and true MAN.
Blessed be the name of JESUS.
Blessed be JESUS in the most holy Sacrament of His Body and Blood.
Blessed be the HOLY SPIRIT, our strengthener and guide.
Blessed be the great Mother of GOD, Mary most holy.
Blessed be GOD in His angels and in His saints.
Blessed be GOD.
        The Divine Praises, Roman Catholic Benediction of the Blessed Sacrament

The word was made flesh
and dwelt among us.   John 1.14, AV

In him was life, and the life was the light of all people. The light shines
in the darkness, and the darkness did not overcome it.

                                        John 1.4, 5, NRSV

He became what we are
so that we might become what He is.   Saint Irenaeus (*c.* 200)

Also pages 45–6.

Fridays

Jesus Christ our Saviour
The Cross, the Resurrection and Ascension

Song of Christ the King

You CHRIST are the KING OF GLORY,
the eternal SON OF THE FATHER.
When You took our flesh to set us free
You humbly chose the Virgin's womb.
You overcame the sting of death
and opened the kingdom of heaven to all believers.
You are seated at GOD's right hand in glory.
We believe that You will come and be our judge.
Come then, LORD, and help Your people,
bought with the price of Your own blood,
and bring us with Your saints
to glory everlasting.

Te Deum: Part 2, Other Canticles, *CW* [1]

Readings:

It was the third hour when they crucified Him . . . and with Him they
crucified two thieves . . . And at the ninth hour JESUS cried with a
loud voice . . . 'My GOD, my GOD, why have You forsaken Me?' . . . and
. . . gave up His spirit. And the Centurion, who stood by Him . . . said
'Indeed this man was the SON OF GOD'.   See Mark 15.25

CHRIST died for our sins . . . He was buried . . . He was raised on the
third day according to the Scriptures. He appeared to Peter; then to
the Twelve; then He appeared to above five hundred brethren at once,
most of whom are still alive . . . CHRIST has been raised from the
dead, the first-fruits of those who have fallen asleep . . . as in Adam all
die, so also IN CHRIST shall all be made alive.   See 1 Corinthians 15.3

Blessed be the hour, O CHRIST, in which You were born,
    and the hour in which You died;
Blessed be the dawn of Your rising again,
    and the high day of Your ascending:
O merciful and mighty Redeemer CHRIST,
    let all times be the time of my presence with You.
    and of Your dwelling in me. Amen.   Anon.

I am Alpha and Omega, the Beginning and the End.
I am THE LIVING ONE! I was dead,
but now I AM ALIVE for evermore.   See Revelation 1.17

Also pages 48–9 and 50–1.

Saturdays

Looking forward to the Sunday Eucharist

HOLY SPIRIT,
breathe into me the eager desire
to meet the RISEN CHRIST at His Eucharist tomorrow.
As He so lovingly invites me
to share His Risen life
    at that holy Meal, that Sacrament and Sacrifice,
may I be there without fail, because He is expecting me.   HO

O COME to my heart, LORD JESUS,
there is room in my heart for Thee.

From 'Thou didst leave thy throne' by Timothy R. Matthews (1826–1910)

The apostle Saint Paul said:

The Cup of blessing which we bless, is it not the Communion of the
BLOOD OF CHRIST? The Bread which we break, is it not the
Communion of the BODY OF CHRIST? . . . But let a man examine
himself and so let him eat of that Bread, and drink of that Cup . . .

1 Corinthians 10.16, 11.28, AV

CHRIST was the Word that spake it
He took the bread and brake it
and what His word doth make it
that I believe and take it.

Queen Elizabeth I

O HOLY SPIRIT, show me all my sins of thought, word and deed or
neglect, which I have committed since my last Communion: and grant that
I may be truly sorry and receive CHRIST's forgiveness. Amen.

(Be honest to GOD about your sins)

Cleanse me, O GOD OUR FATHER, from all my sins and secret faults, that
OUR LORD JESUS CHRIST when He comes may find in me a mansion
prepared for Himself.

As a watchman looks for the morning, so do I look for You, O
CHRIST: come with the dawning of the day, and make Yourself known to
me in the Breaking of Bread. Amen.

Anon.

Also pages 74, 84 and 90.

Joy at Christ's Incarnation (The Angelus)

Dawn, mid-day, sunset – or once a day

The Angel of the Lord brought tidings to Mary
and she conceived by the Holy Spirit.

Hail Mary, full of grace, the LORD is with you.
Blessed are you among women,
and blessed is the fruit of your womb, JESUS.
Holy Mary, Mother of God, pray for us sinners,
now, and at the hour of our death.

'Behold, the handmaid of the LORD:
Let it be to me according to Your word.'
Hail Mary . . .

The word was made flesh
and dwelt among us.
  Hail Mary . . .

Pray for us, O holy Mother of GOD,
that we may be worthy of the promises of CHRIST.

Let us pray:

We beseech You O LORD,
to pour Your grace into our hearts;
that as we have known the Incarnation
of Your SON JESUS CHRIST
by the message of an angel,
so by His cross ✠ and passion
we may be brought to the glory of His resurrection;
through JESUS CHRIST OUR LORD. Amen.   11th century

Joy at Christ's Resurrection (Regina Coeli)

From Easter to Trinity, instead of the Angelus, say:

Joy to you, O Queen of Heaven, alleluia,
He, Whom you were meet to bear, alleluia,
As He promised, has arisen, alleluia,
Pour for us to Him your prayer, alleluia!

V. Rejoice and be glad, O Virgin Mary, alleluia!
R. For the LORD has arisen indeed, alleluia!

Let us pray:

O GOD, who by the Resurrection of Your SON, OUR LORD JESUS CHRIST,
has given joy to the whole world: Grant that with the prayers of His
Mother the Virgin Mary, we may obtain the joys of everlasting life; through
the same CHRIST OUR LORD. Amen.

✠ May the DIVINE ASSISTANCE remain with us always, and may the souls
of the faithful departed, through the mercy of GOD, rest in peace. Amen.

Traditional

VARIOUS THINGS
TO PRAY AND PONDER

GOD
the Sacred Trinity

About prayer when busy

Think often of GOD when you are busy working or enjoying yourself, as well as when you are relaxing. In this way you will share with Him your everyday life, with all its joys and sorrows.

GOD is always with you, even when you are not aware of Him. He is always interested in you. He always loves you, no matter what happens, no matter what you do.

So do not ignore GOD in your everyday life, just as you would not ignore a great friend who came to see you. GOD does not expect much from you – a little thinking of Him from time to time, a little loving attention to Him, sharing with Him your everyday life. The briefest matter-of-seconds thought of Him will be acceptable to Him.

You can do this any time, any place, whether you are alone or with others. You can do this without words – just a secret loving look at Him. You can do this in short, sharp, secret prayers which you make up or which you know by heart.

Based on an excerpt from The Practice of the Presence of God
by Brother Lawrence (d. 1691)

Days of discipline and self-denial

ASH WEDNESDAY, GOOD FRIDAY.
The other weekdays in LENT.
Every Friday in the year (except all Principal Feasts and Festivals outside Lent and Fridays from Easter to Pentecost).

Rules to Order the Christian Year, *CW* [1]

Father, whose SON JESUS CHRIST
fasted forty days in the wilderness,
and was tempted as we are, yet without sin;
give us grace to discipline ourselves
    in obedience to Your SPIRIT:
and, as You know our weakness,
so may we know Your power to save;
through our SAVIOUR JESUS CHRIST. Amen.

Collect for First Sunday in Lent (adapted), *CW* [1]

Fasting means cutting out or cutting down on food.
Abstinence means no meat, or a charitable act.

Personal prayers

CHRIST be with me, CHRIST within me,
    CHRIST behind me, CHRIST before me,
CHRIST beside me, CHRIST to win me,
    CHRIST to comfort and restore me.
CHRIST beneath me, CHRIST above me,
    CHRIST in quiet, CHRIST in danger,
CHRIST in hearts of all who love me,
    CHRIST in mouth of friend and stranger.
                    St Patrick's Breastplate

May the Cross ✠ of the SON of GOD,
which is mightier than all the hosts of Satan,
and more glorious than all the hosts of Heaven,
abide with me in my going out and coming in,
    by day and by night, at morning and at evening,
at all times and in all places may it protect and defend me.
    From the wrath of evildoers, from the assaults of evil spirits,
from foes visible and invisible, from the snares of the devil,
from all passions that beguile the soul and body;
may it guard, protect and deliver me. Amen.
                    Indian prayer

JESU, Son of the Virgin pure,
guide me through this life,
May Your love be in all my thoughts,
    Your likeness in my face.
For love of You
    may my heart warm to others
    who are warm hearted to me
    and to those who are not.
Be with me always, by day, by night,
    by night, by day.
                    Gaelic prayer

LORD GOD, our beginning and our end
You were with me at my birth,
   be with me through my life;
You are with me through my life,
   be with me at my death;
and because Your love and mercy will not leave me then,
   help me pass through death
   and rise to everlasting life with You
   and all whom I love. Amen.
                                                Anon. (adapted)

Soul of CHRIST, sanctify me:
Body of CHRIST, save me:
Blood of CHRIST, invigorate me:
Water from the side of CHRIST, wash me:
Passion of CHRIST, strengthen me:
Cross of CHRIST, protect me:
Good JESU, hear me:
Within Your wounds, hide me:
Never let me be separated from You:
From the deadly enemy, defend me:
In the hour of my death, call me
And bid me come to You,
That with all Your Saints I may praise You
For ever and ever. Amen.
                              Anima Christi, 14th century

Following Christ

CHRIST my SAVIOUR,
give me grace to grow in holiness,
deny myself, take up my cross
and follow You faithfully all my days. Amen.
                                     See Matthew 16.24

Anger, bitterness, evil thoughts

Father, may Your HOLY SPIRIT
take from me all anger and bitterness,
and all evil thoughts that assault and hurt the soul:
for JESUS' sake. Amen.
                                               Anon.

The tongue

Set a watch, O LORD, upon my tongue:
that I may never speak the cruel word, which is untrue;
or, being true, is not the whole truth;
or being wholly true, is merciless;
for the love of JESUS CHRIST OUR LORD. Amen.

George Briggs (d. 1959), Canon of Worcester

For drivers

Father, may Your HOLY SPIRIT
guide and protect (me) this day,
that (I) may travel safely without any mishap
and not cause accident, injury or death
to any living creature,
for JESUS' sake. Amen.   HO

LORD, make me an instrument of Your peace.
    Where there is hatred, let me bring love:
    where there is injury, forgiveness:
    where there is discord, unity:
    where there is error, truth:
    where there is doubt, faith:
    where there is despair, hope:
    where there is darkness, light:
    where there is sadness, joy.

Divine Master
    help me not to seek so much
    to be consoled as to console:
    to be understood, as to understand:
    to be loved, as to love.

For it is giving that we receive:
    it is in forgiving that we are forgiven:
    it is in dying that we are born again
    to eternal life.   After St Francis of Assisi

Time and space for God

The essence of prayer is GOD, who gives Himself to us all the time, whether we are aware of it or not. The essence of life, or the point of life, is to be united to GOD, and we can only do that as we allow GOD space in our lives to 'pray in us'.

When we set aside time to pray, GOD comes to us at the depth of our being, beyond conscious experience, so that He can clothe us head to foot in His holiness.

But our time of prayer, whether it is personal or corporate, is not a time when we 'perform' in order to please GOD, but a time when we come to Him in our spiritual poverty, our lack – ready to let love do its work in us . . . Prayer truly is GOD's work – all we can do is allow GOD the time and space to be about His business.

Matthew Carlisle, Priest in the Manchester Diocese
CR Quarterly, *2006*

I stand at the door and knock.
If anyone hears My voice and opens the door,
I will come in and eat with them,
and they with Me.   Revelation 3.20 (adapted)

Centred on God

Made in the image of GOD, our role now, and our goal is, fellowship with Him . . . Our goal is a growing likeness to GOD in doing His will, a growing fellowship with Him: but mingled throughout with a growing dependence upon Him in reverence and awe, for He is our Maker no less than our Friend . . . We exist in order that we may become like GOD, be united with GOD, 'give glory' to GOD. This is sometimes called 'worship' . . . it means loving GOD above all else for the perfection that is His but, because He is perfect love, our love for Him is reflected in our love and our practical service of our fellows in community. But, because it is His gift, and we are utterly dependent upon Him, our love for our fellows brings us back again to 'give glory' to GOD – the source of all good, the essence of all good.

Michael Ramsey (d. 1988), 100th Archbishop of Canterbury, 1961–1974

Bowing at the name of Jesus

The ancient custom of bowing the head whenever the Name of JESUS is mentioned is a physical act of humility and worship, and a visible sign that we love and serve Him as our LORD and SAVIOUR.

Done simply and silently without fuss, it can also be an act of Christian witness when 'JESUS' and 'JESUS CHRIST' are used by very many as terms of abuse, mockery and blasphemy on TV, radio, in books, popular entertainment and everyday speech.

There is no other Name under heaven granted to mankind by which we may receive salvation.   See Acts 4.12

The sign of the Cross

The sign of the Cross ✠ is made with the right hand from the forehead to the chest, and from the left shoulder across to the right.

We were marked with CHRIST'S Cross at our Baptism:

1 *As a visible reminder to all that* we belong to CHRIST, not ourselves – 'CHRIST claims you for His own. *Receive the sign of the Cross.'*

2 *And that we must* 'not be ashamed to confess the faith of CHRIST crucified'.

From very early Christian times most Christians have made the sign of the Cross ✠ as an outward and visible sign of inward and spiritual prayer or desire to GOD – a prayer involving physical action at the beginning and ending of a time of praying, when receiving forgiveness or a blessing, in times of crisis or danger: 'At every going in and out . . . in all the ordinary actions of daily life, we trace upon the forehead the Sign of the Cross'. (Tertullian, c. AD 200)   HO

Petitions

Those near and dear to me

Father of mercies, I pray for all whom I love . . .
for Your love for them is greater than mine,
and You want for them only what is for their good.
So have them in Your keeping, O LORD,
and give them now and always the blessing of Your peace,
for JESUS CHRIST's sake. Amen.   Anon.

LORD GOD, I trust You not for myself alone,
but for those also whom I love
now hidden from me by the shadow of death; (especially . . .);
for, as I believe You raised
OUR LORD JESUS CHRIST from the dead,
so I trust You to give eternal life to all who believe in Him;
Who is alive and reigns with You and the HOLY SPIRIT
ONE GOD, now and for ever. Amen.   Anon.

The sick

Almighty Father, giver of life and health:
look mercifully on the sick and suffering (especially . . .)
that by Your blessing on them and those who care for them,
they may be restored to health, if it is best for them;
through JESUS CHRIST OUR LORD. Amen.   Anon.

The incurable

Heavenly Father, look in mercy on all who are beyond human help,
all whose hope is gone; all whose sickness finds no cure, (especially . . .).
Give them Your strength, O GOD, to endure with courage and patience,
Knowing that You are with them to bring good out of evil;
Life out of death;
through JESUS CHRIST OUR SAVIOUR. Amen.   Anon.

Refugees

GOD the Father of all, I ask Your mercy
for the refugees of many nations, (especially . . .)
    for the sick, the homeless, the starving and the lonely,
    and for those separated from family and friends.
Direct the minds of statesmen, and the charity of all people,
to the relief of their sufferings and the healing of their sorrows;
through JESUS CHRIST OUR LORD. Amen.   Anon.

World peace

The twentieth century saw millions of human beings exterminated because they were different – Armenians by the Turks, Kulaks by Stalin, Jews by Nazis, Tutsis by the Hutus in Rwanda, Cambodians by Pol Pot, and Albanians, Serbs and Croats in the former Yugoslavia, Shi'ites and Sunnis in Iraq. 'Ethnic cleansings' still go on, as do the horrendous killings by fanatical terrorists.

O GOD, lead us from death to life;
from falsehood to truth.
Lead us from despair to hope,
from fear to trust.
Lead us from hate to love,
from war to peace.
Let peace fill our hearts, our world, our universe. Amen.

Satish Kumar, adapted from the Upanishads

Persecuted Christians

Two hundred million Christians in more than sixty countries suffer from the most brutal persecution because they are Christians. They are under pressure to reject CHRIST and to convert to some other religion or atheism. More than forty-five million Christians were exterminated in the twentieth century.

This is so from militant Muslim zealots in Afghanistan, Algeria, Azerbaijan, Bangladesh, Brunei, Chechnya, Egypt, the Holy Land (Israel/Palestine), Indonesia, Iran, Iraq, Lebanon, Libya, Maldives, Pakistan, Qatar, Somalia, Sudan, Turkmenistan, Uzbekistan, Yemen, etc., and British Christians converted from Islam; from militant Buddhist zealots in Bhutan, Sri Lanka, etc.; from militant Hindu zealots in India; from militant atheist/secularist zealots in Burma, Cuba, China, Laos, North Korea, Turkey, Vietnam, etc.

Few know of this in the West. Governments, political leaders and parties, TV, newspapers, public opinion 'do not do GOD' and keep silent. Nothing is done to protect these our relatives in CHRIST. They need our prayers and compassionate help. We must not forget them. We must not desert them.

Information taken from the Sunday Times Magazine, *27 May 2007*
(a rare exception to the usual silence of the media)

Father, I pray for all persecuted Christians (especially . . .).
In Your mercy may their afflictions soon cease.
Give them strength to endure for CHRIST'S sake,
   courage to continue witnessing to CHRIST,
   and grace to pray for their tormentors.
May their sufferings and deaths not be in vain,
   Your Church strengthened by adversity,
   and Your Gospel commended to all people,
   especially their tormentors:
for the sake of our crucified and risen SAVIOUR, JESUS CHRIST. Amen.

HO

Animals

Father in heaven, I thank You for all living things
which You have made, and especially for the animals of Your creation.
Give to all who deal with them a heart of compassion,
that no dumb creature may suffer cruelty or fear at our hands,
and keep us always thankful for their faithful companionship
and service, through JESUS CHRIST OUR LORD. Amen.   *Anon.*

For all animals cruelly and violently ill-treated:
– those kept in cages and all in captivity
– those misused in scientific experiments
– those misused in factory farming
– those misused in animal baiting
– those misused in transportation by land, sea or air
– the hunted, lost or hungry
– those taken to slaughter
LORD, have mercy.   *Anon.*

Renewal of a church or religious community

*There are some 16,000 churches and thirty-eight religious communities of men
and women in the Church of England, with some eighty branch houses.*

Father, may (. . .) be renewed in all things
by the power of Your HOLY SPIRIT.
Give it a fresh vision of Your glory.
May it grow in numbers, in godly discipline
and true holiness, in unity and peace;
that it may be more fit for Your purpose:
through JESUS CHRIST OUR LORD. Amen.   HO

The Church

Father in heaven, I thank You
for Your Family the Holy Catholic Church,
and for that part of it in which you have placed me,
    the Church of England.
By the unseen working of Your HOLY SPIRIT
make it strong, where it is weak:
make it humble and compassionate, where it is powerful:
where it is corrupt, purify it:
make it holy, where it is worldly:
re-convert it, where it has lost the vision of Your glory:
protect it, where it is persecuted:
resurrect it, where it has died:
and may it soon spread to where it has not yet reached:
for JESUS's sake, who created it.   HO

Although there are many seasons of dryness and darkness in the history of the Church, although Christian people have sometimes been on the verge of despair, yet when they least expected it, fresh springs arose in the desert, and 'through the scent of water it was able to bud, and it brought forth boughs like a plant'.

No church historian has yet given us a study of the way in which 'renewal' comes to the Church. Yet we do not need to be great scholars to know that again and again, when the life of the Church was at a very low ebb, some new element intervened and changed the whole situation. *From the purely human point of view these periods of renewal are inexplicable . . .*

In every case, this 'new life' emerges from a praying group . . . *In other words, the 'living water' comes from* CHRIST HIMSELF, where two or three meet in His name – *and where, as in the first community in Jerusalem,* they remain steadfastly together in faith and fellowship, in sacramental life and prayer. *For 'renewal' always comes when we return to the source, to JESUS CHRIST HIMSELF.*

But all through the course of the history of the Christian Church, this return to the source means going into the 'desert'. It is there in the solitude and silence, that the voice of GOD is heard; it is there that the river of prayer is born, that prayer which is the life-blood of the Church.   *Olive Wyon*

In any need or trouble

LORD JESUS CHRIST,   *or*   Holy GOD
Son of GOD,   holy and strong,
have mercy on me,   holy and immortal,
a sinner.   have mercy upon me.

Confessions (adapted), CW [1]

The JESUS PRAYER and the TRISAGION above can be repeated over and over again, silently or aloud, in our need.

There is no place where GOD is not,
wherever I go there GOD is.
Now and always He upholds me with His power,
and keeps me safe in His love.

Anon.

O LORD, hear;
O LORD, forgive;
O LORD, hear me and act;
Delay not.

See Daniel 9.19

LORD GOD, even though today seems cheerless, dark with trouble,
my work dreary, and my strength weak,
deep down within me there is a ray of light, a ray of hope.
    I know my greatness, for I belong to You.
You have chosen me, called me,
and given me a place in Your heart.
I live safely in the circle of Your care.
I cannot for a moment fall from Your protecting arms.
I am on my way to glory with You
through the joys and sorrows of everyday life. Amen.   Gaelic prayer (adapted)

LORD JESUS,
by the loneliness of Your suffering on the cross
　　be near to me in my need.
Banish my fears,
increase my faith;
hold me in Your love
　　and fill me with Your peace;
　　for Your Name's sake. Amen.　　　　　　　　　Anon.

Why are you so full of heaviness, O my soul
　　and why are you so disquieted within me?
O put your trust in GOD
for I will yet give Him thanks,
　　who is the help of my countenance, and my GOD.

Psalm 42, The Psalter, *CW* [1]

Let nothing disturb you:
let nothing frighten you:
all things pass:
GOD never changes.
Patience achieves
　　all that it strives for.
Those who have GOD
　　find they lack nothing.
Only GOD meets all their needs.　　St Teresa of Avila (d. 1582), Spanish mystic

CHRIST be with me, CHRIST within me,
　　CHRIST behind me, CHRIST before me,
CHRIST beside me, CHRIST to win me,
　　CHRIST to comfort and restore me.
CHRIST beneath me, CHRIST above me,
　　CHRIST in quiet, CHRIST in danger,
CHRIST in hearts of all who love me,
　　CHRIST in mouth of friend and stranger.　　St Patrick's Breastplate

JESUS said:

Come to Me, all you that are weary and are carrying heavy burdens
and I will give you rest.　　　　　　　Matthew 11.28, NRSV

O LORD, I call to You; come to me quickly;
hear my voice when I cry to You.   Psalm 141, The Psalter, *CW* [1]

The LORD is near to the brokenhearted
and will save those who are crushed in spirit.   Psalm 34, The Psalter, *CW* [1]

Fear not, for I have redeemed you
I have called you by name: you are Mine.   Isaiah 43.1, RSV

Where can I go then from Your spirit?
   Or where can I flee from Your presence?
If I climb up to heaven, You are there;
   if I make the grave my bed, You are there also.
If I take the wings of the morning
   and dwell in the uttermost parts of the sea,
even there Your hand shall lead me,
   Your right hand hold me fast.
If I say 'Surely the darkness will cover me
   and the light around me turn to night;
Even darkness is no darkness with You;
   the night is as clear as the day;
darkness and light to You are both alike.'   Psalm 139, The Psalter, *CW* [1]

The LORD is my shepherd
therefore can I lack nothing.
He shall feed me in a green pasture
and lead me forth beside the waters of comfort.
He shall convert my soul
and bring me forth in the paths of righteousness, for His Name's sake.
Yea, though I walk through the valley of the shadow of death,
   I will fear no evil
for Thou art with me; Thy rod and Thy staff comfort me.
Thou shalt prepare a table before me against them that trouble me
Thou hast anointed my head with oil, and my cup shall be full.
But Thy loving-kindness and mercy shall follow me all the days of
   my life
and I will dwell in the house of the LORD for ever.   Psalm 23, BCP

When sick

LORD, I am weak and ill,
but I know You are with me,
that You love and care for me.
Give me strength to bear it with courage
and, if it is best for me, heal me:
who healed the sick,
and suffered and died and rose from the dead
for us and for our salvation. Amen.   HO

I send love and prayer for what lies ahead.
And **whatever** does lie ahead,
we know that the hands of GOD are around us
and the homecoming to GOD is before us
with the best welcome we can ever imagine.
'Where I AM there shall My servant be also',
and conversely, I think 'Where My servant is,
there I AM also'. GOD'S peace to you.

An Anglican nun, to someone awaiting major heart surgery

JESUS, save me,
Mary and all the saints, pray for me.

JESUS said:

Father! All things are possible for You.
Take this cup of suffering from Me.
Yet not what I want, but what You want.   See Mark 14.36

Father, into Your hands
I commend my spirit.   Luke 23.46, NRSV

Joy in God's Creation

Bless the LORD, O my soul.
O LORD my GOD, how excellent is Your greatness!
You are clothed with majesty and honour,
wrapped in light as in a garment . . .
O LORD, how manifold are Your works!
In wisdom You have made them all;
    the earth is full of Your creatures . . .
When You send forth Your spirit, they are created,
    and You renew the face of the earth.

Psalm 104.1–2, 26, 32, The Psalter, *CW* [1]

How wonderful, O LORD, are the works of Your hands!
The heavens declare Your glory,
the arch of the sky displays Your handiwork.
In Your love You have given us the power
to behold the beauty of Your world in all its splendour.
The sun and the stars, the valleys and the hills,
the rivers and the lakes, all disclose Your presence.
The roaring breakers of the sea tell of Your awesome might;
the beasts of the field and the birds of the air
    proclaim Your wondrous will.
In Your goodness You have made us able
    to hear the music of the world.
The voices of loved ones reveal to us that You are in our midst.
A divine song sings through all creation.

Jewish prayer

GOD my Creator,
You Yourself created my innermost parts;
You knit me together in my mother's womb.
I thank You, for I am fearfully and wonderfully made;
marvellous are Your works, my soul knows well.
My frame was not hidden from You,
when I was made in secret
    and woven in the depths of the earth.
Your eyes beheld my form, as yet unfinished;
already in Your book were all my members written,
as day by day they were fashioned
when as yet there was none of them.   See Psalm 139

Also pages 17–18.

Thanks and praise

O praise GOD in his holiness:
Praise Him in the firmament of His power.
Praise Him in His noble acts:
Praise Him according to His excellent greatness.
Praise Him in the sound of the trumpet:
Praise Him upon the lute and harp.
Praise Him in the cymbals and dances:
Praise Him upon the strings and pipe.
Praise Him upon the well-tuned cymbals:
Praise Him upon the loud cymbals.
Let every thing that hath breath: praise the LORD.   Psalm 150, BCP

For the gift of the SPIRIT;
  Blessed be CHRIST.
For the Catholic Church;
  Blessed be CHRIST.
For the means of grace;
  Blessed be CHRIST.
For the hope of glory;
  Blessed be CHRIST.
For the triumphs of His gospel;
  Blessed be CHRIST.
For the lives of His saints;
  Blessed be CHRIST.
In joy and in sorrow;
  Blessed be CHRIST.
In life and in death;
  Blessed be CHRIST.
Now and unto the end of the ages;
  Blessed be CHRIST.   *Cuddesdon Office Book*

I sought the LORD and He answered me:
He delivered me from all my fears.
In my weakness I cried to the LORD;
He heard me and saved me from my troubles.   See Psalm 34

Praise the LORD, O my soul,
and all that is within me praise His holy Name;
Praise the LORD, O my soul
and forget not all His benefits.   Psalm 103.1–2, BCP

The Holy Incarnation

In the beginning was the WORD,
and the WORD was with GOD, and the WORD was GOD
... all things were made by Him ...
And the WORD BECAME FLESH, and dwelt among us,
Full of grace and truth. John 1.1, 3, 14, RSV (adapted)

O come, all ye faithful, joyful and triumphant,
O come ye, O come ye to Bethlehem;
come, and behold Him, born the King of Angels:
O come, let us adore Him,
O come, let us adore Him,
O come, let us adore Him, CHRIST the LORD.

GOD of GOD, Light of Light,
Lo! He abhors not the Virgin's womb;
Very GOD
Begotten not created:
O come, let us adore Him,
O come, let us adore Him,
O come, let us adore Him, CHRIST the LORD.

Yea, LORD, we greet Thee, born this happy morning;
JESUS, to Thee be glory given;
WORD of the FATHER, now in flesh appearing:
O come, let us adore Him,
O come, let us adore Him,
O come, let us adore Him, CHRIST the LORD. 18th century, trans. F. Oakeley

We believe and declare that our LORD JESUS CHRIST,
the SON OF GOD, is both DIVINE and HUMAN.

As GOD He is equal to the FATHER,
as HUMAN He is less than the FATHER.
Although He is both divine and human
He is not two beings but ONE CHRIST.

For as mind and body form one human being
so the ONE CHRIST is both divine and human.

Athanasian Creed, Authorized Affirmations of Faith, CW [1]

Also pages 19–20.

BEHOLD, a virgin shall conceive and bear a son
and His name shall be called 'EMMANUEL'
(which means 'GOD WITH US')
Matthew 1.23, RSV

We declare our faith in the affirmation of the catholic Creeds that IN JESUS CHRIST, fully GOD and fully HUMAN, the Second Person of the Blessed TRINITY is INCARNATE.

As regards the VIRGINAL CONCEPTION OF OUR LORD, we acknowledge and uphold belief in this as expressing the faith of the Church of England, and as affirming that IN CHRIST GOD has taken the initiative for our salvation by uniting with Himself our human nature, so bringing to birth a new humanity.

The House of Bishops of the Church of England,
The Nature of Christian Belief, 1986

The wondrous cross

When I survey the wondrous Cross
    on which the PRINCE OF GLORY died,
    my richest gain I count but loss,
    and pour contempt on all my pride.

Forbid it, LORD, that I should boast
    save in the Cross of CHRIST MY GOD,
    all the vain things that charm me most
    I sacrifice them to His Blood.

See from His head, His hands, His feet,
    sorrow and love flow mingling down:
    did e'er such love and sorrow meet,
    or thorns compose so rich a crown.

Were the whole realm of nature mine,
    that were an offering far too small:
    love so amazing, so divine,
    demands my soul, my life, my all.

Isaac Watts (d. 1748)

JESUS, by Your wounded feet,
    guide me through this life.
JESUS, by Your nailed hands,
    use mine for deeds of love.
JESUS, by Your pierced side,
    cleanse my desires.
JESUS, by Your crown of thorns,
    destroy my pride.
JESUS, by Your silence,
    shame my complaints.
JESUS, by Your parched lips,
    curb my cruel speech,
JESUS, by Your closing eyes,
    forgive all my sins.
JESUS, by Your broken heart,
    fill mine with love for You.

Cuddesdon Office Book (adapted)

We adore You O CHRIST, and we bless You,
because by Your holy Cross You have redeemed the world.

From Anthem 2, Liturgy of Good Friday, CW [3]

We glory in Your Cross, O LORD,
and praise and glorify Your holy Resurrection:
for by virtue of the Cross
joy has come to the whole world.

From Anthem 4 (adapted), Liturgy of Good Friday, CW [3]

Also pages 21–2.

I AM Alpha and Omega, the Beginning and the End.
I AM THE LIVING ONE! I was dead,
but now I AM ALIVE for evermore.
Revelation 1.17

CHRIST's Crucifixion is depicted here against the background of the city centre of Manchester, with the hill of Calvary on the site of the Cathedral, where day by day CHRIST's sacrificial Death and Resurrection are celebrated at the Eucharist and available to all who turn to Him in faith.

The glorious resurrection

Alleluia! Alleluia! Alleluia!
The strife is o'er, the battle done;
Now is the Victor's triumph won;
O let the song of praise be sung.   Alleluia!

Death's mightiest powers have done their worst;
And JESUS hath His foes dispersed;
Let shouts of praise and joy outburst.   Alleluia!

On the third morn He rose again
Glorious in majesty to reign;
O let us swell the joyful strain.   Alleluia!   17th century, trans. F. Pott

The Easter Anthems

CHRIST our Passover has been sacrificed for us,
    so let us celebrate the feast,
Not with the old leaven of corruption and wickedness:
    but with the unleavened bread of sincerity and truth.

See 1 Corinthians 5.7–8

CHRIST once raised from the dead dies no more:
    death has no more dominion over Him.
In dying He died to sin once for all:
    in living He lives to GOD.
See yourselves therefore as dead to sin:
    and alive to GOD in JESUS CHRIST OUR LORD.   See Romans 6.9–11

CHRIST has been raised from the dead:
    the first fruits of those who sleep.
For as by man came death:
    by man has come also the resurrection of the dead;
For as in Adam all die:
    even so in CHRIST shall all be made alive.   See 1 Corinthians 15.20–22

Glory be to the FATHER, and to the SON: and to the HOLY SPIRIT
As it was in the beginning, is now, and ever shall be:
world without end. Amen.

Adapted from the Easter Anthems, Easter Liturgy, CW ³

Also pages 21–2.

CHRIST has been raised from the dead:
the first fruits of those who sleep.
1 Corinthians 15.20

We affirm our faith in the RESURRECTION of our LORD JESUS CHRIST as an objective reality, both historical and divine, not as a way of speaking about the faith of his followers, but as a fact on which their testimony depends for its truth.

As regards belief that CHRIST'S TOMB WAS EMPTY on the first Easter Day, we acknowledge and uphold this as expressing the faith of the Church of England, and as affirming that in the resurrection life the material order is redeemed, and the fullness of human nature, bodily, mental and spiritual, is glorified for eternity.

The House of Bishops of the Church of England, The Nature of Christian Belief, 1986

The Holy Spirit

O HOLY SPIRIT, LORD of grace,
    Eternal Fount of love,
Inflame, we pray, our inmost hearts
    With fire from Heav'n above.

As Thou in bond of love dost join
    The FATHER and the SON,
So fill us all with mutual love
    And knit our hearts in one.

All glory to the FATHER be,
    All glory to the SON,
All glory, HOLY GHOST, to Thee,
    While endless ages run. Amen.   C. Coffin, trans. J. Chandler, 1837

I will sprinkle clean water upon you,
    and you shall be cleansed from all your uncleannesses.
A new heart I will give you,
    and put a new SPIRIT within you,
And I will remove from your body the heart of stone
    and give you a heart of flesh.
You shall be My people,
    and I will be your GOD.   See Ezekiel 36.25, 26, 28

Come, O SPIRIT OF GOD,
and make within me Your dwelling place and home.
May my darkness be dispelled by Your light,
and my troubles calmed by Your peace;
may all evil be redeemed by Your love,
all pain transformed through the suffering of CHRIST,
and all dying glorified in His risen life. Amen.   *Celebrating Common Prayer*

Defend me, O LORD, Your servant, with Your heavenly grace,
that I may continue Yours for ever,
and daily increase in Your HOLY SPIRIT more and more,
until I come to Your everlasting kingdom. Amen.

Confirmation prayer (adapted), Baptism and Confirmation, *CW* [5]

Also pages 18–19.

When the day of PENTECOST had come, the disciples were all together in one
place. And suddenly a sound came from heaven like the rush of a mighty wind,
and it filled all the house where they were sitting. And there appeared to them
tongues as of fire, distributed and resting on each one of them. And they were
all filled with the HOLY SPIRIT and began to speak in other tongues,
as the SPIRIT gave them utterance.

See Acts 2.1

The fruit of the SPIRIT is *love, joy, peace, long-suffering, kindness, goodness,*
faithfulness, meekness, self-control. See Galatians 5.22

The Holy, Blessed and Glorious Trinity

The Three in One, and One in Three

Holy, Holy, Holy! LORD GOD ALMIGHTY!
Early in the morning our song shall rise to Thee!
Holy, Holy, Holy! Merciful and mighty!
GOD IN THREE PERSONS, BLESSED TRINITY!

Holy, Holy, Holy! All the saints adore Thee,
Casting down their golden crowns around the glassy sea;
Cherubim and seraphim falling down before Thee,
Which wert and art and evermore shall be.

Holy, Holy, Holy! Though the darkness hide Thee,
Though the eye of sinful man Thy glory may not see,
Only Thou art holy, there is none beside Thee
Perfect in power, in love and purity.

Holy, Holy, Holy! LORD GOD ALMIGHTY!
All thy works shall praise Thy name in earth and sky and sea;
Holy, Holy, Holy! merciful and mighty!
GOD IN THREE PERSONS, BLESSED TRINITY!

Reginald Heber (d. 1826), Bishop of Calcutta

Praise GOD, from whom all blessings flow,
Praise Him, all creatures here below,
Praise Him above, angelic host,
Praise FATHER, SON and HOLY GHOST.

Thomas Ken (d. 1711), Bishop of Bath and Wells

The Apostles were Jews, in whom the faith of ONE GOD, eternal and invisible in heaven, was deeply implanted. Having watched all our LORD's work for us, and His way of speaking to His FATHER, they found themselves inevitably paying to Him the same worship equally due to that new power set in their hearts at Pentecost. And they knew that here was in fact no contradiction – no apostasy from their old Jewish faith. In fact they at once began to discover implicit in the Old Testament the same trinitarian truth.

GOD eternal (GOD above us): GOD in history (GOD with us): GOD in the life of each one of us (GOD within us).

It is a short step from this to a slightly more philosophical understanding . . . GOD in His Being, GOD in His Showing (His WORD), and GOD in His working (His Power, His SPIRIT). *Derwas Chitty, Priest, Vicar of Didcot (d. 1961)*

Also pages 15–16.

HOLY, HOLY, HOLY LORD,
GOD of power and might,
heaven and earth are full of Your glory.
Eucharistic Prayer, Holy Communion, CW[1]

This ikon depicts the mystery of the SACRED TRINITY. GOD is not simply the all-powerful MAKER (FATHER) of all that exists, but is equally SAVIOUR (SON, JESUS CHRIST) who identified with us and all Creation in His death on the Cross and Resurrection from the dead, and is equally ENABLER (HOLY SPIRIT) who inspires us to seek fullness of life with GOD.

True and lasting happiness

Christ's way – the Beatitudes

'Happy are those who know they are spiritually poor:
the Kingdom of heaven belongs to them!

Happy are those who mourn:
GOD will comfort them!

Happy are the meek:
they will receive what GOD has promised!

Happy are those whose greatest desire is to do
what GOD requires:
GOD will satisfy them fully!

Happy are those who show mercy to others:
GOD will be merciful to them!

Happy are the pure in heart:
they will see GOD!

Happy are those who work for peace among men:
GOD will call them His sons!

Happy are those who suffer persecution
because they do what GOD requires:
the kingdom of heaven belongs to them!'   See Matthew 5.1

The world's way

Blessed are the proud.
Blessed are the violent.
Blessed are those who prosper at any cost.
Blessed are the unscrupulous.
Blessed are the pitiless.
Blessed are the devious.
Blessed are those who fight.
Blessed are the persecutors of those who get in their way.

Many Christians are tempted by an alternative version to CHRIST'S Beatitudes in a world where the violent often triumph and the devious seem to succeed. Yes, says the voice of evil, they are the ones who win. Happy are they.

But like the first Christians, we have to heed Jesus' call for a choice between 'good and evil, life and death', and to believe what He said, 'no matter how strange it may seem'.

Pope John Paul II, Mount of the Beatitudes, Millennium 2000

The Ten Commandments and Our Lord's summary

The commandments God has given His people

1 I am the LORD your GOD;
   you shall have no other gods but me.
2 You shall not idolize anything GOD has made.
3 You shall not dishonour
   the Name of the LORD your GOD.
4 Remember the Lord's Day and keep it holy.
5 Honour your father and your mother.
6 You shall not murder.
7 You shall not commit adultery.
8 You shall not steal.
9 You shall not give false evidence.
10 You shall not set your heart
   on anything that belongs to your neighbour.   See Exodus 20.2–17

OUR LORD JESUS CHRIST'S summary of these laws

1   *Our LORD JESUS CHRIST said: The first commandment is this:*

You shall love the LORD YOUR GOD
with all your heart, with all your soul,
with all your mind, and with all your strength.

2   *The second is this:*

Love *your neighbour* as yourself.

There is no other commandment greater than these.   See Mark 12.30, 31

JESUS said:

Love your enemies, do good to those who hate you,
bless those who curse you, pray for those who abuse you.

Luke 6.27–28, RSV

For me the teachings of CHRIST and my personal accountability before GOD
provide a framework in which I try to lead my life.

Queen Elizabeth II, Christmas Broadcast, 2001

We thank Thee, LORD, Who by Thy SPIRIT doth our faith restore.
When we with worldly things commune and prayerless close our door,
we lose the precious gift divine to worship and adore.
Then Thou, O SAVIOUR, fire our hearts to love Thee evermore.

Princess Margaret (d. 2002)

You did it for me

JESUS said:

Whenever you did this for one of the least important of these My brothers, you did it for ME! . . . Whenever you refused to help one of these least important ones, you refused to help ME! See Matthew 25.40, 45

When I was homeless, you opened your doors,
when I was naked, you clothed Me,
when I was hungry, you fed Me,
when I was tired, you helped Me find rest,
when I was anxious, you calmed My fears,
when I was little, you taught Me to read,
when I was lonely, you gave Me your love,
when I was in prison, you came to My cell,
when I was sick, you cared for My needs,
in a strange country, you made Me at home,
seeking a job, you found Me employment,
hurt in battle, you bound up My wounds,
searching for kindness, you held out your hand,
when I was Black, or Chinese, or White,
mocked and insulted, you carried My cross,
when I was old, you bothered to smile,
when I was restless, you listened and cared,
you saw Me covered with spittle and blood,
you knew My features, though grimy with sweat,
when I was laughed at, you stood by My side,
when I was happy, you shared My joy.   Mother Teresa of Calcutta (d. 1997)

I saw a stranger,
I welcomed him into my home
and put food and drink on the table.
In the Name of the SACRED TRINITY,
He blessed myself, my dear ones, and my home.
And the lark sang in her song –
    Often, often, often,
    goes the CHRIST in stranger's guise.
    Often, often, often,
    goes the CHRIST in stranger's guise.   Gaelic poem (adapted)

One Holy Catholic and Apostolic Church

The Church's one foundation
   Is JESUS CHRIST her LORD;
She is His new creation
   By water and the Word:
From Heav'n He came and sought her
To be His holy Bride,
With His own Blood He bought her,
And for her life He died.

S. J. Stone (1810–76)

O GOD, most glorious and bountiful,
accept my praise and thanksgiving
for Your Holy Catholic Church,
   the mother of us all who bear the NAME OF CHRIST;
for the faith which it has conveyed safely to our time;
and for the mercies by which it has enlarged
and comforted the hearts of men,
for the virtues which it has established upon earth,
and the holy lives by which it glorifies
   both the world and You;
to whom, O BLESSED TRINITY, be ascribed
all honour, might, majesty, and dominion, now and for ever. Amen.

Lancelot Andrewes (d. 1626), Bishop of Winchester (adapted)

The unity of all Christian people

JESUS said:

'I pray . . . that they may all be one;
even as You, FATHER, are in ME, and I in You . . .'

See John 17.21

By Your power LORD,
gather together the scattered flock of Your SON:
that the design of Your love may be accomplished
and that the world may know You, the one true GOD
and JESUS CHRIST whom You have sent.

Abbé Paul Coutourier, French Catholic priest (d. 1953), 'The Apostle of Christian Unity'

We are the BODY OF CHRIST.
In the one SPIRIT we were all baptized into one body
Let us then pursue all that makes for peace
and builds up our common life.

Introductions to the Peace, Supplementary Texts, *CW* [1]

Some relevant information worldwide:
Roman Catholics, one billion plus; Eastern Orthodox, 300 million; Oriental Orthodox (Middle East, Africa and India), 50 million; Anglicans, 70 million; Methodists, 60 million; Pentecostalists, 100 million.

Loving God

This does not shut out the love of others, or spoil our pleasure . . . or take the zeal and interest out of life; we find all these things again in a far more perfect way in GOD. If we open the door to GOD, we open the door to everything else – if we shut the door to GOD, we cannot love, or enjoy, or work in the most perfect way.

Mother Millicent Mary (d. 1956), Society of the Precious Blood, Burnham Abbey

When God seems absent

Never mind, go on praying – say your prayers always, even when prayer is like dust and ashes in your mouth. GOD is always with you, however much He may withdraw the sense of His presence from you . . . all this will pass, only go on, faithfully, patiently, bravely.   *Mother Millicent Mary*

Is anyone there?

She felt an extraordinary impulse which had visited her before and which she thought must be as close as she could ever get to a religious experience. She was possessed by a need, almost physical in its intensity, to pray, to praise, to say thank you, without knowing to whom, to shout with a joy that was deeper than the joy she felt in her own physical well-being and achievements or even in the beauty of the physical world.

P. D. James, crime novelist, Original Sin, 1994 (emphasis added)

GOD – if You exist – make Yourself known to me.   St Augustine of Hippo

Might atheism be a delusion about GOD?

Alister McGrath, Anglican priest, theologian, scientist

GOD is

In the darkness of unknowing
when Your love seems absent,
draw near to us, O GOD,
in CHRIST forsaken,
in CHRIST risen,
our Redeemer and our LORD.

Optional short prayer for use after reciting Psalm 44, CW²

Where I start from as a religious person is not with philosophical paradoxes that ask how can GOD be both all-powerful and all-loving. I start with a sense that there is purpose in existence. That we are connected to SOMETHING bigger than ourselves. That we find greater fulfilment by relating to that, and by seeking the shimmer of transcendence. It is about getting to grips with the mysteries of life.

Paul Vallely, journalist/writer

Death: the gate of eternal life

JESUS said:

I am the Resurrection and the Life. Those who believe in ME, even
though they die, will live. John 11.25, NRSV

I am Alpha and Omega, the Beginning and the End.
I am the living one! I was dead,
but now *I am alive* for evermore. See Revelation 1.17–18

*JESUS had been through death, and that of His own free will. By going through
it He has changed the character of human death. He found it a blind alley; He
made a way through.*

*You know a caterpillar when you see it; and you know it comes from an egg,
and is meant to end up as a butterfly, a vastly better, freer sort of creature. You
know also that your caterpillar cannot develop directly into a butterfly; it must
go through an intermediate stage, that of a chrysalis. It is from the chrysalis that
the perfect insect will in due course emerge. In GOD's economy we human beings
also are metamorphic creatures. From conception to birth we are in the egg
stage. We hatch from that into our present caterpillar stage. Then at death we,
so to speak, turn chrysalis. Till JESUS came, as has been said, death was a blind
alley. Each one who died was like a chrysalis that could not develop, the way was
blocked, the vital force was lacking.*

*But now the way is open, for every one of us who will, to that eternal life
with GOD for which we were created.*

Sister Penelope (d. 1977), Community of St Mary the Virgin, Wantage

*GOD's love and power extend over all creation. Every life, including our own,
is precious to GOD. Christians have always believed that there is hope in death
as in life, and that there is new life IN CHRIST after death.*

Pastoral Introduction, The Funeral, CW [4]

But the souls of the righteous are in the hand of GOD, and no torment
will ever touch them. In the eyes of the foolish they seemed to have
died, and their departure was thought to be a disaster, and their going
from us to be their destruction; but they are at peace.

See Wisdom 3.1–3, 9

Who shall separate us from the love of CHRIST? Shall tribulation or
distress, or persecution, or famine, or nakedness, or peril, or sword?
. . . No, in all these things we are more than conquerors through Him
who loved us. For I am sure that neither death, nor life . . . nor
anything else in all creation, will be able to separate us from the love
of GOD in CHRIST JESUS OUR LORD.   Romans 8.35, 37–39, RSV

ALMIGHTY GOD, I thank You
because through JESUS CHRIST
You have given us the hope of a glorious resurrection,
so that, although death comes to us all,
yet we rejoice in the promise of eternal life;
for to Your faithful people life is changed,
   not taken away,
and when our mortal flesh is laid aside,
an everlasting dwelling place is made ready
   for us in heaven.   Short Proper Preface (adapted) to the
Eucharistic Prayer for a Funeral within Holy Communion, CW⁴

For the dying

Go on your journey from this earthly life,
Christian soul,
   in the Name of GOD our FATHER, who made you;
   in the Name of JESUS CHRIST our SAVIOUR,
   who died and was raised from the dead for you;
   in the Name of the HOLY SPIRIT our GUIDE,
   who strengthened you;
   in company with blessed Mary and all the Saints
   and all the hosts of heaven,
   may you rest this day in peace
   in the heavenly Jerusalem.

Ministry at the Time of Death (traditional, adapted), CW⁴

May CHRIST give you rest in the land of the living
and open for you the gates of Paradise;
may He receive you as a citizen of His Kingdom,
and grant you forgiveness of your sins:
for you are His friend. Eastern Orthodox

HEAVENLY FATHER,
I pray for those whose life is coming to an end,
    especially . . .
    May they know that You are with them,
    that Your love for them
    is stronger than death,
    and that death is *the gate*
    that leads to eternal life with You;
    through JESUS CHRIST our Lord. HO

For those who have died

Think, O LORD, in mercy
on the souls of those
who, in faith gone from us,
now in death repose.
Here 'mid stress and conflict
toils can never cease;
there, the warfare ended,
bid them rest in peace.

Often were they wounded
in the deadly strife;
heal them, GOOD PHYSICIAN,
with the balm of life.
Every taint of evil,
frailty and decay,
good and gracious SAVIOUR,
cleanse and purge away.

Rest eternal grant them,
after weary fight;
shed on them the radiance
of Thy heavenly light.
Lead them onward, upward,
to the Holy place,
where Thy saints made perfect
gaze upon Thy face.

Swahili hymn, trans. E. S. Palmer

Give (*them*), LORD, eternal rest,
and let Your perpetual light shine on (*them*).

Give rest, O CHRIST, to Your servant with the saints:
where sorrow and pain are no more,
neither sighing, but life everlasting.
You only are immortal, the CREATOR and maker of all:
and we are mortal, formed from the dust of the earth,
and unto earth shall we return.
For so You ordained when You created me, saying:
'Dust you are and to dust you shall return.'
All of us go down to the dust,
yet weeping at the grave we make our song:
Alleluia, alleluia, alleluia.
Give rest, O CHRIST, to Your servant with the saints:
where sorrow and pain are no more,
neither sighing, but life everlasting.

Orthodox Kontakion, Ministry at the Time of Death, *CW* [4]

As in Adam all die,
so also IN CHRIST shall all be made alive.

1 Corinthians 15.22, RSV

The LORD gave, and the LORD has taken away;
blessed be the Name of the LORD.

Job 1.21

The Communion of Saints

Have we not at times uncomfortably suspected that it is not so much the saints who are super-human as the rest of us are sub-human: that all men are 'called to be saints', and that 'saint' is but our word for the few who have fulfilled the human destiny . . .? They are what every man was meant to be and would be if he had really been himself.   *Lord Elton*

The Heavenly Hosts
Ye watchers and ye holy ones,
Bright Seraphs, Cherubim and Thrones,
   Raise the glad strain, Alleluya!
Cry out Dominions, Princedoms, Powers,
Virtues, Archangels, Angels' choirs,
   Alleluya, Alleluya, Alleluya, Alleluya, Alleluya!

The Mother of Jesus
O higher than the Cherubim,
More glorious than the Seraphim,
   Lead their praises, Alleluya!
Thou Bearer of the eternal WORD,
Most gracious, magnify the LORD,
   Alleluya, Alleluya, Alleluya, Alleluya, Alleluya!

All Souls and All Saints
Respond, ye souls in endless rest,
Ye Patriarchs and Prophets blest,
   Alleluya, Alleluya!
Ye holy Twelve, ye Martyrs strong,
All Saints triumphant, raise the song
   Alleluya, Alleluya, Alleluya, Alleluya, Alleluya!

The whole Church in earth and heaven
O friends, in gladness let us sing,
Supernal anthems echoing,
    Alleluya, Alleluya!
To GOD THE FATHER, GOD THE SON,
And GOD THE SPIRIT, THREE IN ONE,
    Alleluya, Alleluya, Alleluya, Alleluya, Alleluya!

Athelstan Riley (d. 1945), Anglican layman

No Christian is solitary. Through Baptism we become members one of another in CHRIST, members of a Company of Saints whose mutual belonging transcends death.

Introduction to the Season, All Saints to Advent, CW [4]

The common Christian belief is that we struggling Christians on earth belong to the same family as the faithful Departed in paradise and the Saints in heaven. That family is GOD's Family, The Holy Catholic Church. Therefore our Lord's Family and Friends in the Gospels, and His Saints of later ages, are our relatives – they are fellow-members with us of CHRIST's Body the Church, near to us through CHRIST. They also have a loving concern for us and all that we do. We have, as Saint Paul said, 'this large crowd of witnesses around us'.

The Blessed Virgin Mary is the most highly honoured member of that Family, because she alone was found to be fit to be the Mother of JESUS. Since early Christian times most Christians have thought it right to ask her for her motherly prayers, as they have struggled to follow her Son, our Saviour JESUS CHRIST.

HO

O GOD the King of Saints,
We praise and magnify Your Holy Name
for all Your Servants who have died in Your faith and fear,
for the Blessed Virgin Mary, the Holy Patriarchs,
    Prophets, Apostles, and Martyrs,
and for all Your righteous Servants;
and I ask that, encouraged by their examples,
    strengthened by their fellowship, and aided by their prayers,
we may gain everlasting life in their joyful company;
through YOUR SON, OUR SAVIOUR, JESUS CHRIST. Amen.

Scottish Prayer Book, The Order for the Burial of the Dead (adapted)

ALMIGHTY GOD
by Your HOLY SPIRIT You have made us one
    with Your Saints in heaven and on earth;
grant that in our earthly pilgrimage
we may ever be supported by this fellowship of love and prayer,
and know ourselves surrounded by their witness to Your power and mercy;
through JESUS CHRIST OUR LORD. Amen.

> Prayer for All Saints' Day, Prayer Book of the Episcopal Church of the United States

Mary, the Mother of my LORD,
I thankfully remember your GOD-centred life,
    doing His will in all things, without regard to the cost:
how you were the only one found fit
    to be the means of JESUS becoming one of us:
how you loved and cared for Him,
    and told others to obey Him in all things
how you stood by Him at the Cross,
    and how He loved and cared for you even as He was dying.
As He loved you, may I love you too,
    and follow your advice to obey Him always.
Please pray for me
that I may always be faithful to Him as a member of His Body the Church,
    no matter what the cost.   HO

Silent with God

The Word of God and the Bible

In the beginning was THE WORD. For Christians, the WORD OF GOD is not a written text, the Bible, but the living person of JESUS CHRIST. That is the definitive key to a truly Christian interpretation of the Bible.

Without the Bible, we would not know what JESUS was remembered to have done and said. We would not know the Jewish context of prophetic expectation in which he lived. We would not see how human perceptions of GOD developed from the tribal war-god of the early Hebrew tribes to the GOD of unlimited love who was seen in JESUS. The Bible is an essential text for Christians, and there is something to learn from every part of it..

But much that we learn from the Bible is about human failures to understand GOD, and limitations of vision that were only slowly overcome. In the person of JESUS – healing, forgiving, reconciling, condemning religious arrogance, consorting with the poor, and calling all to the way of love – is our key to interpreting the Bible . . . For Christians, each part of it must be read in a way that points to the fullness of CHRIST.

Keith Ward, Professor of Divinity, Gresham College, London
and Regius Professor of Divinity Emeritus, University of Oxford

GOD speaks to us *through the Bible. Reading the sacred text with the conviction that GOD is speaking to us through this text is known as* lectio divina – *'Godly reading' or 'meditative reading'. GOD is addressing me through the words of Scripture, and I feel moved to address GOD in prayer.*

Choosing a text. *Start with a Gospel (such as St Mark's) in the Bible and read it section by section.* *

Read slowly. *The text is a gift to be accepted, not a problem to be dissected.* Before reading *pray that GOD will speak to you through this text.* After reading *keep some phrase in mind and repeat it throughout the day.*

Guigo, a twelfth-century Carthusian monk, described the process of lectio divina as four movements – reading, meditation, prayer *and* contemplation. *By meditation he means a deep entry into the meaning of the text. By prayer he means the reader's response to GOD in the light of this meaning, and by contemplation he means a simple resting in the presence of GOD, without the need for any further words –* 'Reading, *as it were, puts food into the mouth;* meditation *chews it up;* prayer *extracts its flavour;* contemplation *is the sweetness itself which gladdens and refreshes.' The image of eating is helpful – I am allowing the WORD of GOD into the very fabric of my life and delighting in its presence. In the same way that consuming the bread and wine in the Eucharist is a communion with CHRIST, so reading becomes communion and begins to transform life.*

Based on an excerpt from Finding Sanctuary
by Christopher Jamison, Abbot of Worth, 2006

---

*Or use the Communion Gospels in the Book of Common Prayer, or the readings for the daily services in the *Common Worship* lectionary.

GOD'S FORGIVENESS

About sin and forgiveness

If we say we have no sin, we deceive ourselves and there is no truth in us. But if we confess our sins to GOD . . . He will forgive us our sins and make us clean from all our wrongdoing. If we say we have not sinned, we make a liar out of GOD . . .
See 1 John 1.8–10

A Christian is not one who never sins, but one who when he sins does not lose his confidence in GOD and repents and continues the fight, with the help of GOD's grace. As long as he keeps close to GOD to the best of his ability, never ceasing to hope in GOD, then he will be sure to win in the end, by GOD 's grace.

Anon.

I commend to you what is called 'Going to Confession' or 'Sacramental Confession', the method whereby you confess your sins audibly in the presence of the priest, and receive from him audibly CHRIST's absolution. The Church of England offers this way of Confession and Absolution to those who voluntarily choose it. It is a method thorough, painful, decisive, full of comfort . . . because self has suffered a defeat.

Michael Ramsey (d. 1988), 100th Archbishop of Canterbury, 1961–1974

Our LORD JESUS CHRIST gave power to his Church to forgive sins in His Name. This ministry is exercised by Bishops and Priests. Absolution can be given generally as in the public services of the Church, or individually and privately. The practice of confessing to GOD in the presence of a Priest, under the seal of secrecy, was retained at the Reformation in the Book of Common Prayer and in subsequent revisions of that book. Confession is open to all Christians. Those who fail by themselves to find peace of mind can, if penitent, be assured of GOD's forgiveness through the exercise of this ministry. Here, too, is the opportunity to ask for informed counsel when in doubt or difficulty. The prayers, readings or other devotions which the Priest may ask the penitent to use are suitable expressions of his thankfulness to GOD and his intention not to sin again.

Book of Common Prayer of the Church in Wales (adapted)

I do not know which is the more dangerous to the eternal welfare of a soul, to come to Communion with an uneasy conscience or to stay away for good and all because one cannot quiet one's own conscience. And against either of these dangers the Church of England provides the remedy of private confession . . .

Canon Peter Green (d. 1961), Rector of Saint Philip's, Salford

The LORD is full of compassion and mercy:
long-suffering and of great kindness.
See Psalms 103.8 and 145.8

I had the best of parents, and a good Christian home. I was a Communicant, and had taught in Sunday School – I had lots of enjoyment in my life, but I hadn't got the kind of joy CHRIST spoke about, and I hadn't got the peace of GOD in my heart . . .

One evening in Holy Week I found myself in church where a man was preaching . . . somehow GOD spoke to me that night and showed me that what I needed was to face out my past life more thoroughly than I had ever done before, to examine my life, and then to bring it all out in the open to my SAVIOUR . . .

I spent a good deal of time examining my life from my early days, and I wrote it all down; very ugly it looked in black and white. Then on Easter Eve – I shall never forget that day – I went into church and I knelt down, and told GOD everything – the things I was most ashamed of – in the presence of one of GOD's ministers. I did it in that way, partly because I knew CHRIST has said to His disciples: 'Whosoever sins ye forgive, they are forgiven.' I wanted that message of forgiveness spoken to me personally: thank GOD, I had it; and I can tell you as simply as I know how, that I got up from my knees a different man. The burden of a lifetime had gone; joy and peace became real, and the whole world had become a different place.

Now I knew what those words mean – 'The blood of JESUS CHRIST cleanseth from all sin', and afterwards came a great longing that other people might know what JESUS CHRIST can do for a sinner.

You see, I had believed in a way – I had been baptized, I had been confirmed! I'm very glad I had; but something was blocking up the way, the channel was choked. It wasn't my parents' fault; it wasn't the fault of circumstances; it was my fault. Now through faith and repentance JESUS had touched me and said: 'Be clean', and the HOLY SPIRIT had His chance. Looking back, I can thank GOD who sent that man to disturb my peace . . . to give me CHRIST's peace in the Church.

Brother Edward (d. 1953), Anglican priest and spiritual guide

There can be no disclosure of what is confessed to a priest. This principle holds even after the death of the penitent. The priest may not refer to what has been learnt in confession, even to the penitent, unless explicitly permitted. Some appropriate action of contrition and reparation may be required before absolution is given. A priest may withhold absolution.

From Guidelines for the Professional Conduct of the Clergy

JESUS *said:*

'As My FATHER has sent Me, I am sending you.' And He breathed on them and said, 'Receive the HOLY SPIRIT. If you forgive anyone their sins, they are forgiven: if you do not forgive them, they are not forgiven.'

See John 20.21–23

Approach God

Prepare

GOD is loving and merciful.
He has chosen me to be His own.
He always loves me, even when I turn from Him
    and sin in my self-centredness.
Even then He loves me, and longs for me
to turn back to Him, sorrowing for my sins.
He never ignores anyone who turns to Him.   HO

LORD, You know all about me: nothing is secret from You!
Please help me to see myself as You see me,
    so that I can find out all my sins in Your company,
    be truly sorry for them,
    and confess them to You.
Then turn to me, LORD, and have mercy on me:
forgive all my sins:
and guide me in the eternal life. Amen.   HO

Almighty and everlasting GOD,
who hatest nothing that Thou hast made,
and dost forgive the sins of all them that are penitent;
Create and make in us new and contrite hearts,
that we worthily lamenting our sins,
and acknowledging our wretchedness,
may obtain of Thee, the GOD of all mercy,
perfect remission and forgiveness;
through JESUS CHRIST our LORD. Amen.

Collect for Ash Wednesday, BCP

Be honest with God

Think carefully and honestly about yourself, admitting to yourself all your sins, great and small. Write your sins on paper so you won't forget them or try to hide them,

First write down the sins that come immediately to your mind. Then use the list below to remind you of other sins you may have forgotten or refuse to think about. (Destroy the list after your Confession.)

Don't just say vaguely: 'I've been bad' – say how you have been bad. Don't accuse yourself of things you haven't done; and don't name or blame other people. It's your sins you're bothered about.

You shall love the Lord your GOD with all your heart, and with all your soul, and with all your mind, and with all your strength. Mark 12.30

Do I love GOD most of all? . . . Do I let anything else take His rightful place in my life – myself, someone else, work, sex, money, pleasure, getting on, etc.? . . . Do I miss meeting Him at His Eucharist *every* Sunday and *every* main Holy Day, for no good reason? . . . If I miss the Eucharist on any of these days, do I pretend it doesn't matter? . . . Am I reverent in church, or do I stop others and myself from concentrating on GOD by needless talking and whispering? . . . Do I just trip to the altar for Holy Communion without thinking WHO I am going to meet and receive in the Holy Sacrament? . . . Do I receive the Holy Sacrament of CHRIST's Body and Blood when I am full of hatred and bitterness? . . . Do I pray with GOD every day? . . . Am I a prayer-less Christian? . . . Do I welcome strangers in church, or do I make them feel unwelcome and unwanted? . . . Does Sunday shopping keep me from the Sunday Eucharist? . . . Is my churchgoing just one hobby among others? . . . Or is it an awesome and loving meeting with GOD IN CHRIST?

Love your neighbour as yourself. See Mark 12.31

Do I love, respect, and help my family (parents, wife, husband, children, etc.)?. . . Is home-life a hell because of me? . . . Do I spend sufficient time with my family? . . . When things go wrong at work or elsewhere, do I vent my anger on my family? . . . Is my family against GOD and His Church because of me? . . . Do I set a disciplined and loving example in Christian worship and life to my family? . . . Does my family come before GOD? . . . Is my family too closely knit, too inward looking, and unfriendly to others? . . .

Do I regard my sexual impulses as a gift from GOD or as a necessary evil? . . . Am I obsessed with sex, making it the centre of my life? . . . Do I use my sexual impulses only in a loving relationship? . . . Am I faithful to my wife or husband? . . . Do I interfere in other people's marriages? . . .

Do I hate anybody? . . . Am I jealous of anybody? . . . Do I brood over real or imaginary hurt? . . . Am I unwilling to forgive anybody? . . . Is my tongue a vicious weapon, which deeply hurts others by lying, slandering and malicious gossip? . . . Have I hurt anybody physically? . . . Is anyone's life a living hell because of me? . . . Do I enjoy causing trouble? . . . Do I make 'bullets for others to fire', and then remain quietly in the background? . . . Do I meddle in other people's private affairs? . . . If I dislike anyone, do I still try to want what is best for them? . . . Am I cruel to animals, which are made by GOD like me? . . .

Do I keep myself to myself, aloof, unfriendly and unwelcoming to others? . . . Am I too exclusive in my friendships? . . . Am I a loyal friend? . . . Is my group of friends a troublesome clique? . . .

Do I show the love and compassion of CHRIST to the lonely, the old and the sick? . . . To those who are despised, mocked, rejected and persecuted by other (minority groups, real or imaginary sinners, social misfits, people of another race or colour, etc.) . . . Do I react to them like JESUS, who when a crowd was intending to stone to death an adulterous woman, said: 'Let he who has never sinned throw the first stone'? . . . Am I narrow-minded, bigoted, hard-hearted, unloving, snobbish or unsociable? . . . Am I a good neighbour to all in genuine need? . . . Do I pretend that evil is good, or that good is evil? . . .

Do I do a fair day's work for a fair day's pay? . . . Do I remember that I must answer to GOD regarding my work? . . . Do I want money for nothing, not working hard enough or doing my work carelessly and badly? . . . Am I ruthless in business? . . . Does money count more than people in my life and work? . . . Am I harsh to those under me? . . . Do I make a god out of my work, neglecting GOD and my family and others because of it? . . . Do I pick and steal? . . .

Am I a 'flash in the pan', full of enthusiasm for the latest new thing, but soon losing interest and letting others down by breaking promises and trust? . . . Do I keep my promises to GOD and His Church and others? . . .

Do I take on more paid or unpaid work than I can cope with? . . . If unable to do anything I have promised to do, do I admit it and resign quickly and quietly without fuss? . . . Or do I hang on in a spirit of martyrdom, waiting to find some excuse so that I can resign, blaming others? . . . Am I too busy? . . . Do I have enough time off from work to worship GOD, enjoy my family, and rightfully rest and enjoy myself? . . .

Do I think I am too good to need forgiving by GOD or anyone else?

Do I think I am too bad to be forgiven by GOD or anyone else?

Do I hate myself? . . . Do I hate GOD? . . .

It is a fearful thing to come before the unutterable goodness and holiness of GOD, even for those who are redeemed IN CHRIST . . . it is searing as well as life-giving to experience GOD's mercy.

Introduction to the Season, All Saints to Advent, CW [3]

Have mercy on me, O GOD, after Your great goodness;
for I acknowledge my faults, and my sin is ever before me.
Turn Your face from all my sins, make me a clean heart, O GOD,
and renew a right spirit within me.   See Psalm 51

Confess to God

The Reconciliation of a Penitent

This may be appropriately used when a person's conscience is burdened with a particular sin, when a person wishes to make a new beginning in the Christian life, or as part of a regular personal discipline.

Introductory Note (adapted), Reconciliation of a Penitent, CW[5]

Short Confession and Absolution

Priest: May the LORD be in your heart and on your lips, that you may make a true confession of your sins, in the Name of the FATHER, and of the SON, and of the HOLY SPIRIT. Amen.

You say: I confess to ALMIGHTY GOD, and before you, that I have sinned through my own fault. I remember especially the following sins . . .

For these and all my other sins, which I cannot now remember, I am very sorry; I firmly resolve not to sin again, and humbly ask pardon of GOD, and of you counsel and absolution in His Name.

The priest may now give counsel, if required, and ask the penitent to use an appropriate devotion.

Priest: Our LORD JESUS CHRIST, who has left power to His Church to absolve all sinners who truly repent and believe in Him, of His great mercy forgive you all your offences. And by His authority committed to me, I absolve you from all your sins, in the Name of the FATHER, and of the SON, and of the HOLY SPIRIT.

You say: Amen. Thanks be to GOD.

Priest: The LORD has put away your sin.
Go in peace; and pray for me a sinner.

Book of Common Prayer of the Church in Wales

Note: The Church of England provides fuller forms of Confession and Absolution in Common Worship: Christian Initiation: *The Reconciliation of a Penitent.*

Thank God

Happy are those whose sins are forgiven,
whose transgressions are pardoned.
I confessed my sins to YOU:
I did not conceal my wrongdoings.
I decided to confess them to YOU,
and You forgave all my transgressions.

See Psalm 32

Thank you, merciful GOD,
for loving me when I turned against You:
for so lovingly forgiving all my sins
    when I turned back to You.
All the old godless things are cleared away:
    now everything is new and clean.
For You have forgiven all my sins,
    I have passed from death to life,
        to new and better life with You.
    For You have said to me
        through Your priest,
Be happy! All your sins are forgiven.

HO

HOLY SPIRIT, now that I am free from my sins,
    help me to make a fresh start
        in following CHRIST all my days.
    Help me to conform to CHRIST,
        outwardly and inwardly,
        in all things,
    so that I become completely transformed
into His likeness, for Your glory.

HO

Let us celebrate with a feast!
Because this child of mine was dead,
   but now is alive:
   was lost,
   but now has been found.

See Luke 15.32

JESUS said:

There will be more joy in heaven over one sinner who repents, than over ninety-nine righteous persons who need no repentance.

Luke 15.7, RSV

The unworthiness of the ministers . . . hinders not the effect of the Sacrament.

Article 26 of the Thirty-Nine Articles of the Church of England

GOD'S FORGIVENESS

AT THE EUCHARIST

THE LORD'S OWN SERVICE
HOLY COMMUNION, MASS OR
LORD'S SUPPER

When to go to the Eucharist

1 WORSHIP AT THE EUCHARIST at least on:

Easter Day and
All Sundays in the year, and

Main Holy Days, such as:

Christmas Day *(25 December)*	Good Friday *(the Liturgy of the Passion)*
The Epiphany *(6 January)*	The Ascension Day
The Annunciation *(25 March)*	Corpus Christi
Ash Wednesday	Feast of the Virgin Mary *(15 August)*
Maundy Thursday	All Saints Day *(1 November)*

2 RECEIVE HOLY COMMUNION always at:

Easter, Whitsunday (Pentecost), Christmas and regularly at other times after preparation. Don't just trip to the altar unthinkingly or with a bad, unforgiven conscience.

If anyone eats the LORD's Bread or drinks from His Cup in a way that dishonours Him, he or she is guilty of sin against the LORD'S BODY AND BLOOD. So then, you should all examine yourselves first, and then eat the Bread and drink from the Cup. For if people do not recognize the meaning of the LORD'S BODY when they eat the Bread and drink from the Cup, they bring judgment on themselves as they eat and drink.

See 1 Corinthians 11.27–29

You then, who truly and earnestly repent of your sins,
and are in love and charity with your neighbours,
and intend to lead a new life,
following the Commandments of GOD,
and walking from this day forward in His holy ways:
draw near with faith,
and take this Holy Sacrament to your comfort;
and make your humble confession to Almighty GOD.

Invitation to Confession, Holy Communion, Order Two (Contemporary), *CW* [1]

If you are serious in following CHRIST and being united with Him, then nothing except serious illness or some serious cause will ever keep you away from your meeting with Him at His Eucharist on all Sundays and other main Holy Days. If the weather is good or bad or indifferent, if you are at home or away, if you are busy with work or pleasure, if you are tired out or full of life or bored, whether it is convenient or not, if you feel like it or not – you will be there at the Eucharist without fail to meet OUR LORD JESUS CHRIST. He has invited you, and He is expecting you.   *HO*

Before the Eucharist

Be silent and still with GOD. Do not talk or whisper, concentrate on GOD. Use whatever of these prayers are helpful – or just be silent with GOD.

As a deer desires the water-brooks
so longs my soul for You, O GOD.
My soul thirsts for GOD,
Yes, even for the living GOD.
See Psalm 42

LORD JESUS CHRIST,   *or*   HOLY GOD,
SON OF GOD,   holy and strong,
have mercy on me,   holy and immortal,
a sinner.   have mercy upon me.   *CW*[2]

The JESUS PRAYER or the TRISAGION above can be repeated over and over again, silently.

Father, may Your HOLY SPIRIT
take from me all anger and bitterness,
and all evil thoughts that assault and hurt the soul:
for JESUS' sake. Amen.
Anon.

Master, lover of mankind, LORD JESUS CHRIST, my GOD,
do not let these Holy Mysteries be for my condemnation
because of my unworthiness
but for the cleansing and sanctification of my soul and body. Amen.
Eastern Orthodox prayer

I am not worthy, O LORD, to receive You into myself:
> but since You desire to dwell in me,

I despair not of my salvation,
> and make bold to draw near

> to receive these Holy and Life-giving Mysteries.

As You did not despise the sinful woman who came to You with tears,
> nor reject the tax-gatherer when he repented,

nor spurn the penitent thief when he hung with You on Calvary,
> and reckon all who come to You in penitence as Your friends:

> even so, LORD JESUS, receive me.

JESUS CHRIST, SON OF GOD, have mercy on me, a sinner.

Eastern Orthodox prayer

LORD, I come to this Eucharist
with other faithful Christians
> – for Your honour and glory . . .

> – in thanksgiving for all Your mercies . . .

> – for the forgiveness of my sins . . .

> – for the good of all mankind . . .

> – for the good of the whole Church . . .

> – for my family, friends

and all I ought to pray for, living and departed . . .
> – and for myself, with all my hopes and fears . . .   HO

Give us, LORD CHRIST,
the fullness of grace,
Your Presence and Your very Self,
for You are our portion and our delight,
now and for ever.

Optional short prayer for use after reciting Psalm 16, CW ²

Going to the altar
to meet Our Lord

Our LORD JESUS CHRIST is present in the Holy Sacrament on the altar for you to meet and receive Him.

JESU, Son of Mary,
LORD of life alone,
here we hail Thee present
on Thine altar-throne.
Humbly we adore Thee,
LORD of endless might,
in the mystic symbols,
veiled from earthly sight.

Swahili hymn, trans. E. S. Palmer

Blessed and praised be JESUS CHRIST
in the most Holy Sacrament.
Hosanna, Hosanna,
Hosanna in the highest.

As you go to the altar to meet and receive JESUS in the Holy Sacrament repeat silently, over and over again:

O come to my heart, Lord JESUS:
there is room in my heart for Thee.

or

**LORD JESUS CHRIST, SON OF GOD
Have mercy on me, a sinner.**

See Luke 18.38

After receiving
Holy Communion

Back in your place, be thankful, *be* silent *or repeat silently over and over again:*

JESU MY LORD, I Thee adore:
O make me love Thee more and more.

My LORD, and my GOD.   John 20.28

LORD, You are in me, and I in You.

At the end of the Eucharist

Thank you, LORD, MY GOD,
because You have not rejected me a sinner,
but have counted me, the unworthy,
worthy to share in Your most pure and heavenly Gifts.

Eastern Orthodox prayer

All praise to You, our GOD and FATHER,
for You feed us with the Bread of Heaven,
and quench our thirst from the True Vine
– our risen Saviour, JESUS CHRIST.

Post Communion (adapted), Corpus Christi, *CW* [3]

CHRIST be with me, CHRIST within me,
   CHRIST behind me, CHRIST before me,
CHRIST beside me, CHRIST to win me,
   CHRIST to comfort and restore me,
CHRIST beneath me, CHRIST above me,
   CHRIST in quiet, CHRIST in danger,
CHRIST in hearts of all who love me,
   CHRIST in mouth of friend and stranger.

St Patrick's Breastplate

If anyone is IN CHRIST, there is a new creation:
the old has passed away; everything has become new!

See 2 Corinthians 5.17–19a

You are Christians! Then your LORD is one and the same with JESUS on His throne
of glory, with JESUS in His blessed Sacrament, with JESUS received into your hearts
in Communion, with JESUS who is mystically with you as you pray, and with JESUS
enshrined in the hearts and bodies of His brothers and sisters up and down the
world.

   Now go out into the highways and hedges, and look for JESUS in the ragged
and naked, in the oppressed and sweated, in those who have lost hope, and in
those who are struggling to make good. Look for JESUS in them; and when you
find Him, gird yourselves with His towel of fellowship, and wash His feet in the
person of His brethren.   *Frank Weston (d. 1924), Bishop of Zanzibar,*
extract from speech to the Anglo-Catholic Congress, 1923 (adapted)

Do this in remembrance of me

JESUS told His friends to do this, and they have done it always since. Was ever another command so obeyed? For century after century, spreading slowly to every continent and country and among every race on earth, this action has been done, in every conceivable human circumstance, for every conceivable human need, from infancy and before it, to extreme old age and after it; from the pinnacles of earthly greatness to the refuge of fugitives in the caves and dens of the earth.

Men have found no better thing than this to do for kings at their crowning and for criminals going to the scaffold; for armies in triumph, or for a bride and bridegroom in a little country church; for the wisdom of the Parliament of a mighty nation or for a sick old woman afraid to die . . . for the settlement of a strike; for a son for a barren woman; for Captain so-and-so, wounded and prisoner of war; while the lions roared in the nearby amphitheatre; on the beach at Dunkirk; while the hiss of scythes in the thick June grass came faintly through the windows of the church; tremulously, by an old monk on the fiftieth anniversary of his vows; furtively, by an exiled bishop who had hewn timber all day in a prison camp near Murmansk; gorgeously, for the canonization of St Joan of Arc – one could fill many pages with the reasons why men have done this, and not tell a hundredth part of them.

And best of all, week by week and month by month, on a hundred thousand successive Sundays, faithfully, unfailingly, across all the parishes of Christendom, the pastors have done this just to make the 'plebs sancta dei' – the holy common people of GOD.

Dom Gregory Dix (d. 1952), Benedictine monk of the Church of England

Holy Communion *is the sacrament in which, according to CHRIST's command, we make continual remembrance of Him, His passion, death and resurrection, until His coming again, and in which we thankfully receive the benefits of His sacrifice.*

The outward and visible sign in Holy Communion
The outward and visible sign in Holy Communion is bread and wine given and received as the LORD commanded.

The inward and spiritual gift in Holy Communion
The inward and spiritual gift in Holy Communion is the Body *and* Blood *of* Christ, *truly and indeed given by Him and received by the faithful.*

What is meant by receiving the Body and Blood of Christ
Receiving the Body and Blood of Christ *means receiving* the life of CHRIST HIMSELF, *who was crucified and rose again, and is now alive for evermore.*

Revised Catechism of the Church of England

JESUS said:

I am the Living Bread which came down from heaven; if anyone eats this bread they will live for ever: This bread is My flesh, which I will give for the life of the world . . . whoever eats My flesh and drinks My blood has eternal life, and I will raise them up at the last day.

See John 6.51, 54

I am the True Vine . . . you are the branches. Whoever abides in Me, and I in them, shall bear much fruit: but apart from Me you can do nothing.

See John 15.1, 4, 5

The Eucharist *is the only service or offering to GOD which our SAVIOUR commanded us to do. It is therefore far more important than any other church service; it is the centre of our Christian life. It is not a fringe benefit or optional extra. He began it at His last supper with His friends when He told them, 'Do this in memory of Me.'*

JESUS with us
Although present and accessible everywhere to anyone who turns to Him, JESUS has chosen to focus His real presence under the signs of the bread and wine of the Eucharist, which He said are His Body and Blood. So we rightly worship JESUS really and truly present under the signs of the bread of His Body and the wine of His Blood.

'In memory' of JESUS
He used the term 'in memory' not in the modern sense of thinking about a past event, but in the old Jewish sense of making present and real now a past event, so that we can share in it now. JESUS *is not a past event – He is very much alive now. But in the Eucharist He makes present* now *all that He did for GOD's glory and our salvation in His whole GOD-centred sin-free life on earth and especially at His Birth, Death, Resurrection and Ascension.*

The one true sacrifice

A sacrifice is life offered completely to GOD. The whole life of JESUS was the one human life offered completely to GOD – it was what all human life is meant to be, centred not on self but on loving GOD and others. His whole life was therefore a successful battle against evil – that hateful, merciless and destructive power, which feeds on our self-centredness, separates us from GOD and one another, and creates the miseries of human life and death.

This battle against evil reached its climax in His suffering and death on the Cross – and He was shown to have won the once and for all victory over evil suffering and death when GOD raised Him from the dead.

We share in all this in the Eucharist – the way JESUS chose to share with us His Sacrifice and Victory, so that through HIM, in the power of the HOLY SPIRIT, we may be united to GOD our Father – and also be united to all who belong to Him in His Body the Church on earth, in paradise, and in heaven. The Eucharist therefore contains all that our Christian Faith is about. It is of Divine appointment and perpetual obligation. HO

The Christian hope

A Christian lives in the certain hope of the Advent of CHRIST, *the Last Judgement and Resurrection to Life Everlasting.*

By the advent of CHRIST, *we are to understand that* GOD, who through CHRIST has created and redeemed all things, will also through CHRIST at His coming again make all things perfect and complete in His eternal kingdom.

By the last judgement, we are to understand that all people will give account of their lives to GOD, who will condemn and destroy all that is evil, and bring His servants into the joy of their LORD.

By resurrection, we are to understand that GOD, who has overcome death by the resurrection of CHRIST, will raise from death in a body of glory all who are CHRIST's, that they may live with Him in the fellowship of the saints.

Our assurance as Christians is that neither death, nor life, nor things present, nor things to come, shall be able to separate us from the love of GOD, which is in JESUS CHRIST our LORD. *Thus,* daily increasing in GOD's HOLY SPIRIT, and following the example of our Saviour CHRIST, we shall at the last be made like unto Him, *for* we shall see Him as He is.

May the GOD of all grace,
who has called us unto His eternal glory by JESUS CHRIST,
    after that we have suffered awhile,
make us perfect, stablish, strengthen, settle us.
To Him be glory and dominion for ever and ever. Amen.

Revised Catechism of the Church of England

CHRIST IS THE MORNING STAR

WHO WHEN THE NIGHT OF THIS WORLD IS PAST

BRINGS TO HIS SAINTS

THE PROMISE OF THE LIGHT OF LIFE

AND OPENS EVERLASTING DAY

Inscription near tomb of the Venerable Bede, Durham Cathedral

Acknowledgements

The compiler wishes to express his gratitude for permission kindly given to include copyright material in this book.

Every effort has been made to seek permission to use copyright material reproduced in this book. The compiler and publisher apologize for those cases where permission might not have been sought and, if notified, will formally seek permission at the earliest opportunity and ensure that full acknowledgements are made in a subsequent reprint or edition of this book.

Illustrations

The compiler wishes to express his gratitude to Sister Theresa Margaret CHN for permission to reproduce six ikons made by her and also for the other drawings made especially for this book. They are here not just for decorative purposes but as focal points to meet GOD in prayer. The ikon on page xiii is in St Barnabas, Ealing: that on page 49 is in Manchester Cathedral and those on pages 53 and 55 respectively are in the Convent Chapels of CHN Derby and of SSC at Tymawr Convent, Gwent.

Bibles

Extracts from the Authorized Version of the Bible (The King James Bible), the rights in which are vested in the Crown, are reproduced by permission of the Crown's Patentee, Cambridge University Press.

Scriptures quoted from the Good News Bible published by The Bible Societies/HarperCollins Publishers Ltd UK are copyright © American Bible Society, 1966, 1971, 1976, 1992, 1994.

Scripture quotations taken from the HOLY BIBLE, NEW INTERNATIONAL VERSION. Copyright © 1973, 1978, 1984 by International Bible Society. Used by permission of Hodder & Stoughton Publishers, a member of the Hachette UK Group. All rights reserved. 'NIV' is a registered trademark of International Bible Society. UK trademark number 1448790.

Scripture quotations from the New Revised Standard Version of the Bible, Anglicized Edition, are copyright © 1989, 1995 by the Division of Christian Education of the National Council of the Churches of Christ in the USA. Used by permission. All rights reserved.

Scripture quotations from the Revised Standard Version of the Bible are copyright © 1946, 1952 and 1971 by the Division of Christian Education of the National Council of the Churches of Christ in the USA. Used by permission. All rights reserved.

Prayer books and liturgies

Extracts from *The Alternative Service Book 1980* are copyright © The Archbishops' Council and are reproduced by permission.

Extracts from The Book of Common Prayer, the rights in which are vested in the Crown, are reproduced by permission of the Crown's Patentee, Cambridge University Press.

The Book of Common Prayer of the Church in Wales (Canterbury Press).

'For the gift of the Spirit' and 'Jesus, by Your wounded feet', from the *Cuddesdon Office Book*. Reproduced by kind permission of the Principal of Ripon College Cuddesdon.

Extract from the Scottish Prayer Book, 1929 (updated 1987) is used with the permission of the General Synod of the Scottish Episcopal Church.

Common Worship, Guidelines for Professional Conduct of the Clergy and The Revised Catechism

Extract from *Common Worship: Christian Initiation* (Church House Publishing) are copyright © The Archbishops' Council, 2006 and are reproduced by permission.

Extract from *Common Worship: Daily Prayer* (Church House Publishing) are copyright © The Archbishops' Council, 2005 and are reproduced by permission.

Extracts from *Common Worship: Pastoral Services* (Church House Publishing) are copyright © The Archbishops' Council, 2000 and are reproduced by permission.

Extracts from *Common Worship: Services and Prayers for the Church of England* (Church House Publishing) are copyright © The Archbishops' Council, 2000 and are reproduced by permission.

Extracts from *Common Worship: Times and Seasons* (Church House Publishing) are copyright © The Archbishops' Council, 2006 and are reproduced by permission.

The texts of the Apostles' Creed and Te Deum Laudamus as they appear in *Common Worship* are copyright © The English Language Liturgical Consultation and are reproduced by permission of the publisher.

Extract from *Guidelines for the Professional Conduct of the Clergy* (Church House Publishing) is copyright © The Convocations of Canterbury and York 2003 and is reproduced by permission.

Extracts from The Revised Catechism of the Church of England are copyright © The Central Board of Finance of the Church of England 1982, the Archbishops' Council 1999 and are reproduced by permission.

Hymns

Athelstan Riley, 'Ye watchers and ye holy ones', *The English Hymnal* (Oxford University Press, 1933).

Other publications

Matthew Carlisle, excerpt beginning 'The essence of prayer is God', *CR Quarterly*, 2006. Reproduced by kind permission of the Community of the Resurrection, Mirfield.

'Come, O Spirit of God', in David Stancliffe and Brother Tristam SSF (eds), *Celebrating Common Prayer* (Continuum, 2003). Reproduced by permission of Continuum International Publishing Group.

The Community of St Mary the Virgin, Wantage: permission from the late Sister Penelope to reproduce adaptations she kindly made from her book *Your Sorrow*.

Dom Gregory Dix, 'Do this in remembrance of me', from *The Shape of the Liturgy* (Continuum, 2000). Reproduced by permission of Continuum International Publishing Group.

House of Bishops, *The Nature of Christian Belief* (Church House Publishing, 1986).

P. D. James, *Original Sin* (Faber & Faber, 1994).

Christopher Jamison, excerpt from *Finding Sanctuary* (Phoenix, 2007).

Mother Millicent Mary, 'Loving God' and 'When God seems absent', in Sr Felicity Mary SPB, *Mother Millicent* (Society of the Precious Blood, Burnham Abbey, 1968). Reproduced by kind permission of the Society of the Precious Blood, Burnham Abbey.

Mother Teresa, 'Love to pray' and 'When I was homeless', in Malcolm Muggeridge, *Something Beautiful for God* (Collins/Fontana Books, 1972). Reproduced by permission of HarperCollins Publishers.

Michael Ramsey, *Introducing Christian Faith* (SCM Press, 1961). Copyright © SCM Press 1961. Used by permission.

Princess Margaret, prayer, *Church Times*, 2002. Reproduced by permission of the *Church Times*.

Stephen Smalley, extract from a letter on prayer to *The Times*, 2001.

Paul Vallely, excerpt beginning 'Where I start from as a religious person', *Church Times*. Reproduced by permission of the *Church Times*.

J. Neville Ward, *Five for Sorrow, Ten for Joy* (Epworth Press, 1971). Copyright © Epworth 1971. Used by permission.

Olive Wyon, *The Altar Fire* (SCM Press, 1954). Copyright © SCM Press 1954. Used by permission.